The Wagon Wheel Project

The Wagon Wheel Project

by Dave Engen

Photographs by John Cross

MINNESOTA HERITAGE PUBLISHING

Copyright © 2012 Dave Engen
All Rights Reserved

Reproduction in whole or in part of any portion in any form without permission of the author or publisher is strictly prohibited.

For more information, contact:
Minnesota Heritage Publishing
205 Ledlie Lane, Suite 125
Mankato, MN 56001
www.mnheritage.com

ISBN: 978-0-9850937-2-3

Library of Congress Catalog Number: 2012940519
Published by Minnesota Heritage Publishing

Printed in the United States of America
by Corporate Graphics, North Mankato, MN

First Edition

Photographs by John Cross
Edited by Grace Schreyer
Cover design and layout by Lorie Giefer

This project has been made possible by the Arts and Cultural Heritage Fund through the vote of Minnesotans on November 4, 2008. Administered by the Minnesota Historical Society.

Contents

Acknowledgments	i
Foreword	v
Introduction	1
The Wagon Wheel as a Community Gathering Place	4
Bill Neilsen	9
Wes Otto	11
Paul Sonnek	13
Marty Cassem	15
Jerry Breitkreutz	19
Jean Bauer	21
Carole Milner	23
Joel "Augie" Nickel	25
Kenneth Hardt	29
Ruth Spore	31
Elaine Harkins	33
Dolores Vaubel	35
John Harrington	39
Harry B. Coonce	41
Laurel Garvin	43
Harlan Mehlhop	45
Ted & Cortnee Wilcox	49
Randy Wells	51
Royal Lee	53
Erv Kurth	55
Paul Meyer	59
Frank Brown	61
Bob Browne	63
John Marso	65
Jerry Hansen	69
John Berg	71
Rob Foster	73
Dan Dinsmore & Emily Green	75
John & Kathy Dorn	79
Mark Piepho	81
Eric Anderson	83
Marc Buchanan	85
Michelle Fasnacht	89
Dan Johnson	91
Alissa Haney-White	93
Rebel Miller	95
Denise Premeau	99
Lisa Beck	101
Dave Bottin	103
Brad Walker	105
Lowell & Jean Johnson	109
Sandie Blekestad	111
Tammy Phillips	113
Kenny Dewitte	115
Dennis Bents	119
Don Aaker	121
Jim Pfau	123
Jerry Schuck	125
Kevin Haefner	127
Wagon Wheel Timeline	129
Bullshippers Coffee Group	131
Wagon Wheel Index	133

Acknowledgements

From John and Dave . . .

We couldn't have done this project without the help of a whole lot of people.

Thanks to . . .

    Kevin Haefner for saying yes

    Rebel Miller for getting everything started

    Alissa Haney-White and Lisa Beck for keeping it going

    The Free Press of Mankato for making it real

    Tim Walz for his kind and thoughtful foreword to the book

    Julie Schrader at Minnesota Heritage Publishing for her belief, support, and guidance

    Lorie Giefer and Grace Schreyer for their assistance with the layout and editing of the project

    Jessica Potter, Ben Leonard, and Tom Hagen for their support of the project

    The State of Minnesota and the Minnesota Historical Society for helping finance this project through the Arts and Cultural Heritage Fund

And, of course, thanks to all the Wagon Wheel regulars who participated in and supported the project. We're honored you let us in to your lives and to your café.

From Dave . . .

A great big thanks to my wife, Laura Bemel. Her editorial assistance and insight touched every part of this project. Thanks buddy . . . for your help with the book and everything else.

And thanks to . . .

Ken and Yvonne Engen for raising me in a manner ensuring I would appreciate a place like the Wagon Wheel

Grace and Eddie Engen for being great kids and great company on our trips to the Wagon Wheel

John Biewen at Duke University's Center for Documentary Studies for the training and the encouragement

Minnesota State University, Mankato and the Department of Communication Studies for their support of this work—special thanks to Dr. Leah White for seeing things I occasionally miss, and to Dr. Jane Earley and Dr. Walter Zakahi for their support

Jessica Potter at the Blue Earth County Historical Society for helping get me interested in the history of Mankato's Front Street, and Shelley Harrison of the Blue Earth County Historical Society for her help researching the history of the Wagon Wheel

Phil Molling, Amanda Hatling, Julia Dugas and Tanner McLean for their hard work transcribing—thanks to Tanner McLean for his help editing Frank Brown's profile

Stephen Bloom, Peter Feldstein, Michael Perry, John Prine, David Isay, Robert Coles and Studs Terkel for producing some of the remarkable work inspiring this project

Dave and Doris Boyce for teaching me about Front Street and much more

Thanks to good friends Tom McCarthy, Scott Johnson, Troy Murphy, Mary Beth Collery, Bill Miller, Corlyn Miller, Kate Cady, Pravin Rodrigues, Tony Esposito, Dean Abanilla, Robert Jersak, David Viscoli, Kim Musser, Mark McCullough, and Lisa Perez, for supporting this work in all kinds of ways

And finally, thanks to all the good folks I've met in third places around the country who helped me learn to see and hear what really matters

From John . . .

Thanks of course, goes to my wife, Nancy, who over the last 39 years has put up with the uncertain schedules, odd hours, and the strange phone calls that come from being married to a newspaper photographer.

And thanks to . . .

> James and Robert Vance, long-departed brothers who published my hometown paper, the *Worthington Daily Globe*, and were committed to producing the best of community photojournalism and responsible photojournalists
>
> Dr. R. Smith Schuneman, my college professor and advisor at the University of Minnesota's School of Journalism, whose knowledge, insight and patience I now wish I would have appreciated far more than I did as a student
>
> Albert and Agnes Cross who indulged their son's interest in photography and allowed him to spend a foolish sum of money on a first camera so many years ago
>
> *The Free Press*, which provided the first venue for *Wagon Wheel Stories*, and staffers Jenny Malmanger and Josie Belina, who embraced the extra duty to make sure every one of them looked great

Foreword

Walking into the Wagon Wheel, I am reminded of the best of America. This small, unpretentious, warm downtown café is a reflection of who we are. A place where we can all come together to share a meal and share our stories from all walks of life.

I first heard about this compilation of history while having lunch with some campaign volunteers during my 2010 campaign. As a teacher and a lover of history, I was struck immediately by the brilliance of this idea and became excited about the stories that would be collected. Of course, when Professor Engen asked me to write the foreword, I was honored.

My wife Gwen and I first started coming to the Wagon Wheel when we moved to Mankato and began teaching at Mankato West High School, just a few blocks away. Oftentimes, we would stop by the Saturday morning after a Friday night football game. To this day, I usually run into a few former students every time I stop by.

Walking into the Wagon Wheel without seeing someone you know is practically impossible. On the rare occasion you step inside and don't see a familiar face at the tables, it is safe to assume the folks inside are just friends you haven't met yet.

My first stop is usually to see Kevin behind the grill, and if it's spring or summer, he'll have a comment about how the Twins are playing. If it's fall or winter, you can count on a comment about how he's just waiting for the Twins season to start.

I would be remiss if I didn't also mention that the waitresses play one of the most important roles in making this place such a gem. Their welcome smiles make you feel like family.

The unique thing about the Wagon Wheel is the way it appeals to all age groups and people from all walks of life. That attribute is what makes a book like this possible, and it is also what inspires me. As someone who works every single day in the political arena where partisan bickering is at an all-time high, I love being reminded that what unites us is far greater that what divides us.

In a world where the way we connect with people is changing constantly and is increasingly becoming less personal, the Wagon Wheel is a rare place where people still interact face-to-face. And in a world where people become famous for how much money they have or how ridiculous they can be on reality TV, this café is where American stories are still told. Where hard work counts for something and doing right by your families and your neighbors is a strongly held value. And in an ever-changing world, this is a place you can count on.

The stories and photographs in this book will move you. You will identify with the characters, get a kick out of their honesty, experience their pain and their triumph. Most of all, you will learn what this community treasure means to them, and in the process, you just might discover what it means to you.

–Tim Walz,
currently serving in the U.S. House of Representatives, representing the First Congressional District of Minnesota. He has served in Congress since 2007.

Introduction

From John Cross . . .

Having worked as a photojournalist on daily newspapers for more than four decades, it is not in my photographic DNA to delve into in-depth, prolonged projects. By their very nature, newspapers generate assignments where daily deadlines loom and where the rewards are immediate but fleeting. We have a saying in the newspaper business: Today's art, tomorrow's fishwrap.

So my initial reaction to Dave Engen's proposal in February 2010, to collaborate on a book about the Wagon Wheel Cafe, was admittedly measured. While the idea sounded intriguing, undertaking such a project would take no small amount of time and commitment, all to be shoe-horned between my duties at the Mankato *Free Press* and as an adjunct faculty member at Minnesota State University.

But upon further consideration, I began to warm to the idea of documenting the Wagon Wheel and its loyal patrons. First and foremost, the South Front Street business was a Mankato fixture, a neighborhood icon that embodies what community gathering places are all about. It is irreplaceable.

Second, there were the people themselves. People's stories are a journalist's stock in trade, and undoubtedly the wide range of regulars at the Wagon Wheel would have interesting stories and diverse reasons for making the Wagon Wheel a common destination.

Finally, I was impressed by the work Dave had produced as part of his "Voices from the Valley" series and was flattered that he would ask me to be a part of his next project.

The interesting thing about making photographs is that the action itself, a mere split-second of focused light playing across a light-sensitive material, is a mechanical thing. At the click of the shutter, some sort of image will be there.

But any serious photographer knows that it is the time leading up to the decision finally to press the shutter that determines whether the final image hits the mark, especially when people are the subject.

During the two years I spent making photographs for the project, the most rewarding part of the process was being invited into Wagon Wheel customers' homes.

There were the nuts and bolts of photography—the light, the environment, the pose—to consider with each visit, naturally. But a more important and appealing part of each visit was listening to their stories of how they came to regard the Wagon Wheel as a common gathering place.

The Wagon Wheel is a pretty darned good place to eat. Where else in town can one get a complete breakfast, including a bottomless cup of coffee, for five bucks?

But now, with the final digital images committed to some 30 CDs and found throughout this book, to slip into a booth in the Wagon Wheel on a crowded morning with all the now-familiar faces of regulars and staff is to sit among friends.

From Dave Engen . . .

My call to John in February of 2010 came right after I read a book called *The Oxford Project* by Peter Feldstein and Stephen Bloom. The book explored the town of Oxford, Iowa (population 676), through photographs and interviews with residents of the town. I was captivated by the book's exploration of the beauty and complexity of a small community. The book featured short excerpts from interviews with residents of Oxford as well as two photographs of each resident, one taken 20 years ago and one taken today. Almost immediately after reading the book, I began to think about a similar project of photographs and interviews with regulars at the Wagon Wheel Café. As John mentions above, his response was *measured,* but he agreed to a meeting. You're holding the results of that meeting.

Why a book on the Wagon Wheel Café? As a professor of Communication Studies, I have an interest in the topics of community and place. I'm intrigued by the way people come together and through social interaction build something larger than themselves, be that a team, a workplace, or a community. In their writing about the psychological dimensions of community, researchers McMillan and Chavis (1986) explain that a *sense of community* ". . . is a feeling that members have of belonging, a feeling that members matter to one another and to the group, and a shared faith that members' needs will be met through their commitment to be together" (p. 9). It's difficult to spend any time at all in the Wagon Wheel and not notice how this academic definition of community plays out in the café.

Both John and I had spent a good deal of time in the Wagon Wheel before starting this project. Over the years, John has been in to shoot photographs of everything from campaigning politicians to owner Kevin Haefner behind the grill for a newspaper profile of the restaurant. I was a semi-regular before this project started, and I had also done some audio documentary work about the Café and its regulars. In short, we knew the place well enough to know that it was more than the Beef Commercials that keep the business thriving—although the Beef Commercials are indeed awfully good. We wanted to explore in more detail both the regulars of the Wagon Wheel and what the café means to their lives.

Originally our goal was to profile every single regular in the café in the same way as Peter Feldstein set out to photograph every resident of Oxford, Iowa. For a number of reasons, it became apparent profiling every regular would be impossible, as some regulars, despite our charm, preferred not to take part in the project, and the sheer number of regulars (likely well over

100) made it an overwhelming task. We settled on profiling 50 regulars, thinking this a very large cross-section of the collection of characters who frequent the Wagon Wheel. The book you're holding features a total of 55 regulars, four staff and the owner, Kevin Haefner.

Some of the individuals selected for interviews were known by me from my status as a semi-regular of the café. I knew many members of the Bullshippers coffee group, for example, because of an earlier audio documentary I'd completed on the group. In most cases, however, waitresses at the Wagon Wheel would pass along the names of regulars who they thought were important members of the Wagon Wheel community and, frankly, whose arms they could twist into letting us photograph and talk with them. Names of potential participants were passed along to me, most often in the form of a name and number on a guest check. I would then contact these individuals and set up a one-hour interview with the person, typically at the Wagon Wheel but every so often at their homes.

I had only three prepared questions for the interviews: What makes this place special? How do you feel when you walk in the front door? Can you tell me about yourself? Everything else discussed in the interview flowed in a conversational manner, with me saying very little but asking a wide range of questions both about the Wagon Wheel and about the person's life. As you'll see in the pages to follow, the topics that emerged ranged from World War II to how the Wagon Wheel provides comfort to a mother after losing her daughter, from the unique setting the Wagon Wheel provides for a father and daughter's relationship to the sense of accomplishment felt by getting sober. It was not uncommon for individuals to tear up as they talked with me in the Wagon Wheel's trademark orange booths, nor was it uncommon for me to leave the interview feeling I'd made a new friend.

All interviews were recorded and transcribed. The transcripts served as the source for all the stories you will read in the book. Every so often a word or two was changed or added for readability, but never in a way that changed the meaning of what was being said. After each interview, I contacted John with a few highlights and themes from the interview. John then took the information I shared with him and photographed the individual both in his or her home environment and at the Wagon Wheel.

One of my heroes is the late oral historian Studs Terkel, and we did our best to work in the same spirit as Studs. That spirit involves capturing and presenting the stories of "regular" people in a way that reminds us that they are extraordinary. Thirty-one of these stories were published in the Mankato *Free Press* between October 2010 and March 2012. We're proud to present the previously published stories and nearly 20 others here in one place. We invite you to come in, grab a cup of coffee, and enjoy the conversation. Before getting to the people, however, we'd like to to say a few words about the Wagon Wheel Café as a place.

References

Bloom, S. G., & Feldstein, P. (2008). *The Oxford Project*. New York: Welcome Books.

McMillan, D. W., & Chavis, D. M. (1986). Sense of community: A definition and theory. *Journal of Community Psychology*, 14(1), 6-23.

The Wagon Wheel as a Community Gathering Place

Although this project features individuals, it is also a project about a place.

Located at 609 South Front Street, the Wagon Wheel is Mankato, Minnesota's oldest continually operating restaurant. Front Street is significant to this Southern Minnesota town of some 50,000 because it was for years Mankato's commercial hub. Front Street was, for all practical purposes, Mankato's Main Street. The street was largely eliminated from the town during urban renewal in the 1970s, replaced first by a downtown mall and later by government offices and a civic center. The once thriving Front Street talked about by longtime residents—the one with the three dime stores and the department stores and the theatres and the hotels and the homecoming parades—is long gone.

The story here is a familiar one—the commercial hub has moved to the outskirts of town, out by the mall and the Wal-Mart. Yet the Wagon Wheel remains. Indeed, business is thriving. There are many reasons for its success. The food is good, and inexpensive. The place is clean. The location is good, the parking not so much. Ultimately, however, it is the character of the place and the characters in it that make the Wagon Wheel special.

In addition to being the nice small café so many in the Mankato community know and love, the Wagon Wheel is also a nearly perfect example of what sociologist Ray Oldenburg calls a "third place." In his book about third places, *The Great Good Place*, Oldenburg explains that "…daily life, in order to be relaxed and fulfilling, must find its balance in three realms of experience. One is domestic, a second is gainful or productive [work], and the third is inclusively sociable, offering both the basis of community and the celebration of it" (p. 14). For Oldenburg, that third realm of experience comes in the form of what he terms third places, those places between home and work where people gather with a wide variety of others to create and celebrate community. Third places can be places like the neighborhood tavern, the coffee shop, the corner grocery store and, yes, the local café.

Characteristics of a Third Place

Oldenburg contends that third places have eight qualities making them a third place. The qualities are as follows:

A Third Place is on *neutral ground*. A third place is not someone's home and you do not need any kind of membership to enter. A country club, for example, is not a third place because not everyone can walk in and partake in the benefits the country club has to offer.

A Third Place is a *leveler*. A third place is, by definition, inclusive. People from a wide variety of backgrounds come together in a third place, and individuals are judged not because of their occupations or incomes, but on their ability to interact in the third place. It is likely true the leveling process is not perfect, but by definition a third place brings together a true cross-section of a community.

ature*Conversation* is the main activity in a Third Place. People might eat, shop, or have their hair cut in a third place, but one of the main activities is conversation. People come to third places to talk with those in their community.

A Third Place offers *accessibility and accommodation*. It's easy for people to get to a third place. Often, no car is needed, for example. And the third place will do its best to accommodate the needs of its patrons.

A Third Place has *regulars*. There exists in a third place a cast of characters who are there with great consistency. Think here of television's *Cheers*, for example.

A Third Place has a *low profile*. Third places are nice and clean, but, as Oldenburg explains, third places typically "…fall short of the middle-class preference for cleanliness and modernity" (p. 36).

The mood is *playful* in a Third Place. People have fun in third places. They banter with one another, they laugh—they shoot the breeze, if you will.

A Third Place is a *home away from home*. Third places are not homes. But they are often every bit as comfortable as home, sometimes even more so.

There is almost certainly no place that meets all the characteristics of a third place. It is hard to believe, for example, that social distinctions are completely leveled in any one place, nor is any place always fully open to newcomers and the like. That said, the Wagon Wheel Café comes very close to being an ideal third place. We invite you to look for the characteristics of a third place in the pages to follow. To help you make sense of the Wagon Wheel as a third place, we've placed quotations about third places throughout the book. Our hope is to present the Wagon Wheel in a way that both invites you into this specific third place and helps you see and celebrate other third places in your lives.

Reference

Oldenburg, R. (1989). *The great good place: Cafes, coffee shops, community centers, beauty parlors, general stores, bars, hangouts and how they get you through the day*. New York: Paragon House.

"The temper and tenor
of the third place is upbeat; it is cheerful.
The purpose is to enjoy
the company of one's fellow human beings
and to delight in the novelty
of their character…"

Ray Oldenburg—*The Great Good Place*

Bill Neilsen

You meet people from all walks of life in the Wagon Wheel. It is owned and operated by a gentleman—Kevin, Wally's son. Always remember when the Twins lose to go into the Wagon Wheel and ask Kevin if he heard how the game turned out.

I was born in Mankato in 1927 and grew up during the Depression years. These were good years and tough years. Wages were low, but so were prices. It wasn't easy to get head over heels in debt like it is now—neither credit cards or China were available.

My family was a part of the family that operated Neilsen Florist. My first work was in the greenhouse, disbudding carnations. There's something special about the floral business. The smell of flowers. The joy and happiness you see in people's faces when they've got a bouquet of wedding flowers. It feels good to be able to give that to people.

Growing up, I met Catherine Witty of St. Peter. We were 14 and 15 years old when we met. We married in 1949. It was Cathy who introduced me to the Wagon Wheel. She used to work the night shift down here in the late 1950s.

I worked for Hubbard Milling for about 30 years. I was Union President for a good 25 of those. Nobody else wanted the job. I felt like labor needed a voice. Yeah, I've got a lot of feelings over what is happening today to working people. Working people need to have bargaining power, and they're trying to destroy that.

Cathy and I had 57 years together, and I thank God for each one of them. She passed away in 2006 from Alzheimer's disease. I asked God so many times to let me live long enough beyond Cathy so that I could be there for her when she needed me. My life turned out that way.

I cared for Cathy for 12 years as she battled Alzheimer's. The Wagon Wheel was always here for us during that time. I could bring her in here and she could sit down and just be with people, people we loved and respected. We were here every day.

After I retired, I drove school bus for over 20 years. I love those kids. I go to the Catholic church, you know, and I got a couple of them that sing in the choir down there. It's great to see the way they've grown up and what they can do. I'll just never forget those kids, all of them. They made my life, really, is what they did—just by being there. I will admit I was grateful I got hard of hearing so I could turn down my hearing aid sometimes though [laughs].

It's like this is where I belong, you know. The people are here to talk with at the Wagon Wheel—you can solve all the world's problems down here. Well, you can hear all the solutions anyway, let's put it that way [laughs].

Wes Otto

I've been coming to the Wagon Wheel since I could walk. Coming here has improved my ability to communicate with an older generation. When I walk up to one of my friends it's like, *hey dude how's it going*. When I walk in here it's more polite, a little bit more old-school.

I was talking to a guy in here yesterday. I didn't know him at all. He started asking me what school I'm going to and everything. Then I got interested in him so I started asking him what did he do for a living. He used to be a farmer and he also used to have his own trucking business.

It's fun to have interaction with other people and learn things from them. What else am I going to do while waiting for my food? Sit there and read the paper?

I think a lot of people have misconceptions of what 16-year-olds are about, just with our music and who we associate with as far as our pop culture. But overall I think we're going to live, you know what I mean? I don't think we're going to be the generation that destroys the world as some people say. I think we'll be fine.

I try to do as many school activities as I can. I'm in football, wrestling, track, speech, Knowledge Bowl, and the play. I'm also in an organization called FCA, Fellowship of Christian Athletes.

I'm really big into football. As a sophomore I was one of the only people that started and played every single varsity game. My first game was against Lester Prairie. We won 31-0. Right after the game my mom bought me a rather expensive Loyola hat as a memory of my first varsity game. It's still my favorite hat. I keep it in the back window of my car.

I kind of have an idea of going to college here in town. After I graduate college, who knows? In ten years, ideally, I probably won't be in Mankato anymore. Mankato is growing, but I'll be looking for something a little bit bigger by the time I get to that age and that education. I'll probably be working as an executive for some kind of company. Or, if not an executive, then I'll own my own business somewhere in the Twin Cities or in another state. I'd like that.

Paul Sonnek

You develop relationships in this place. Maybe you don't socialize outside of the Wagon Wheel with the people you meet here, but they become part of your life. You come in here and you banter back and forth, you pick on each other a little bit—"Hey Kevin, nice prediction on the game last night," that sort of thing. It's all in jest and it's fun.

You know that young fellow Wes Otto who started his story in the newspaper by talking about how he met this farmer and retired trucker? That was me he was talking about. What amazed me about that young man was that he took an interest in an older person and initiated a conversation with me. Young people just don't seem to do that in today's world.

I don't know if I'd want to start farming today. It used to be a way of life, but it's a business now, that's the way I'd say it. You can't have a family farm when you have a $300,000 combine and a $300,000 tractor. You have to farm thousands of acres to justify that. It's the only way it works. If the government wanted to control agriculture they'd tell John Deere it can't manufacture a tractor that has more than 100 horsepower. If they did that, you'd still have the family farm.

These days everything is about getting big, from farming to retail to restaurants. That's what's so unique about a place like the Wagon Wheel. I grew up in a small town and at one time we had three grocery stores, three restaurants, and a few bars. But that's all gone now.

Along with farming, I was in the trucking business for over 20 years. I drove over the road, and I got involved with owning the trucking company I was working for. I also own a warehouse that we rent out. Not to toot my own horn, but I've also served on and chaired a number of boards over the years, from the Farm Credit Association to the Rural Electric Association and several others. I work hard at everything I do.

I guess one thing that really disturbs me in today's world is there's a word that I think we've lost in society and in business—"accountability." It seems like everybody is suing or it's always somebody else's fault. I've always been in business for myself. If I screwed up, I paid the fiddler. I don't know how you get that accountability back. I really don't know.

What I find special in the Wheel here is its homey atmosphere. The waitresses know you on a first-name basis, and that's a good feeling. Kevin is a personality in and of himself, too. And where else can you have a hamburger and a bowl of soup for $3.36, you know?

Marty Cassem

Editor's Note – Jessica Cassem's comments are in italics.

My daughter Jessica and I started coming to the Wagon Wheel every Friday morning before school about the time she started kindergarten—that was 21 years ago. It was never designed to exclude my wife Mary, who has been very supportive of our coming here. I was just looking for something kind of special where the two of us could spend some time together each week and talk, some special father-daughter bonding time as she started school.

Our Friday mornings went so well that the next child in line, Danielle, joined us two years later when she started kindergarten, and Collin joined us three years after that when he started school.

As kids, we each got a quarter when we came in here, and each week we played the same songs on the jukeboxes in the booths. "Sarah" by Jefferson Starship and "She Talks to Angels" by the Black Crows were two of the ones we always played. Sometimes Geraldine, who works here and is our great-aunt, would come by and toss us a quarter or two and say, "Play a little country western."

Early on I recognized bringing the kids here provided something unique. It's important that the Wagon Wheel is a neutral site. Dad is not in the dominant chair. I would never bring problems to these breakfast meetings, but I allowed the kids to bring theirs and just talk through them. They knew they could kind of say anything here and that they were going to leave in good shape.

The Wagon Wheel is a positive place to be and coming here is something special with our dad. It's a nice little way to touch base at the end of the week and get grounded again.

The conversations have really evolved over the years, from "that little girl down the road is stealing my friends" to "I'm not sure what I should major in at college." In that 16-year-old range, one of them might bring a boyfriend or girlfriend to one of these Friday things. I never asked them to do this or anything, it was always "Dad, can I bring so-and-so?" This allowed me to get to know who they were dating and to watch them interact instead of only getting snippets.

There's drama in families, and over 21 years there have been conflicts on some Thursday nights before we come. But no matter what, we come and we talk. Then Dad stays and pays the bill and we all go on to our days.

All parts of our community are at the Wagon Wheel. We've literally walked around homeless people as we walk in the door, and we know there are very wealthy people who come in here, and everything in between. Over the years, the kids have asked about what they see here, and it's enabled us to have a discussion about how you don't look down on people and you don't have to look way up to people. You find out when you're in a setting like the Wagon Wheel that we're all just part of the community.

How long will this last? I don't know. The idea was that each of the kids would keep coming to these Friday gatherings until they graduated high school. Collin graduates this year and Danielle is away at college in St. Cloud. But Jessica now lives back in Mankato after being away at college for six years, and I know she's going to call after the summer and say, "We're going to breakfast, aren't we?"

"There is a tendency for individuals to select their associates, friends, and intimates from among those closest to them in social rank. Third places, however, serve to expand possibilities, whereas formal associations tend to narrow and restrict them."

Ray Oldenburg—*The Great Good Place*

Jerry Breitkreutz

I like the conversation at the Wagon Wheel. You meet people here. We talk a lot of sports and you can talk to anyone and everyone.

I'm 54 years old, and I come from a family of nine. I was born with cerebral palsy and have been in a wheelchair all my life. I was born a triplet. I have a twin sister and the other one would have been my identical twin brother, but he didn't make it. There wasn't enough oxygen for all of us. That's why he died and why I am the way I am.

I work for MRCI just down the street from the Wagon Wheel. I do payroll. Monday through Friday from 9–2:30. I like the job. If I didn't do anything, I would go crazy looking at the walls, you know. I can't just stay home. That's not me. That's when people get down on themselves.

I lived in a nursing home for a year when I was 18. That's when I really found myself, I guess. I went to live there for my mom and dad. They were looking out for my well-being and said, "Well, if you get sick or whatever, there will always be someone there to help you." But when I was there I kept thinking, "If I live all my life here, I'm going to get old before my time." I worked like hell to get out of there.

I'm always trying to figure out how to better myself. I'm always trying to feel better about situations. I believe the guy upstairs put me on earth this way for a purpose. I believe he wants me to help disabled people, to help the community become more aware of us and to let people like me speak for ourselves, not let people talk for us. Because that drives me crazy—when people try to speak for us. I want to make my own decisions.

People treat disabled people better than they used to. When I used to be in a store I felt like people were staring at me. I felt like I was a freak of nature, you know. Parents would keep their kids away from me. Kids, they're curious and they would say to their parents, "What's wrong with him, how come he's in a wheelchair, how come this and that?" Usually their parents would just grab them by the hand and say, "Get going, don't look at him, just get going." Where now, if kids see me and get curious, more parents let their kids approach me and ask the questions they want to ask. I like that.

To sum everything up, I try to get people to know me as a person. A lot of people misjudge people when they look at someone in a wheelchair. I'm in a wheelchair because I have to be. The wheelchair's not me, but some people think, "Well, he's in a wheelchair, he can't talk, he can't do nothing for himself," you know. They put the wheelchair before me and that's wrong.

I love coming to the Wagon Wheel. People here see more than the wheelchair. It's a good place.

Jean Bauer

I meet friends down at the Wagon Wheel sometimes three times a day. We don't gossip, we just discuss things—the kids, what happened on the weekend, is everybody well and that.

I started working at the American Legion in 1971. People call me "Mean Jean" because I sell the gambling down there and sometimes I'm not too good giving out winners. One guy, when he sees me, he'll say, "Hi Mean," and I don't even hardly sell to him.

My husband and I have been divorced over 30 years. In 2003 he was walking right out here by the Legion with his companion of 25 years. A car hit them. She was killed and he was severely injured. It was a hit and run.

After his sixth fall at his own apartment, he landed in the nursing home for rehab. His brother said, "You're not going back to that apartment, George." But he's deathly afraid of going into nursing homes again. I knew there was no other place for him to go, so I said, "Well, you can come up to the house," that's what I said. So he lives with me now. A lot of people think I'm nuts for having him. They think that because we're divorced I'm not compelled to do this. But he's the father of my children and who else would do it? The kids all work. I've been able to do it. It has been over a year since his last fall.

I'm a lot stronger than people think. When I had my double knee surgery, I came in the room and the doctor said, "Walk to the door." So I did. And he says, "Well, I can see you have a high tolerance for pain." And I do. I don't go to the doctor every time I got a little pain.

About two months ago my son and grandson got me a laptop computer. I thought I'd never be able to work the thing, but I'm hooked. It relaxes me. I lift it up every night and look at the news, and I love playing Solitaire on there. I've played over 1500 games. I was very stupid at first, but now I'm starting to win quite a bit [laughs].

To me the Wagon Wheel is just the greatest place in town. It's homey. You know right away everybody's going to greet you. Kevin has a good clientele down there—a lot of us old buggers.

Carole Milner

I'm a regular. I come here almost five days a week. I have the same thing every day: two eggs—scrambled, bacon, and toast with strawberry jam. You go to another restaurant and you just feel like you're alone. You come here and you don't feel alone. On those days when there's no one to sit and talk with, I just read a book.

I taught emotionally disturbed children for twelve years, first in Illinois, then in Indiana. I left my job in Indiana after nearly ten years. My daughter died and I just couldn't stay there. I moved up to my cabin in Hayward, Wisconsin. I stayed there two years and I thought: *This isn't enough anymore. I need something else.* In 1994 I applied to go to the University of North Dakota to get a Ph.D. and become a college professor.

She was 16 and a half and died in a car accident.

I got a job teaching at Minnesota State. Being a professor is not a job you go to at eight in the morning and you come back at five. It takes up all your time. I don't think I did any of my hobbies when I was working. Nothing. I just taught, read, prepared for classes, graded papers.

I have suffered from depression a lot. It all started after my daughter died. It was really taking a big toll on me. I felt like I had no reason to be because I wasn't carrying on anything for the future. I didn't think I was being an effective professor either. The university put me on disability, and my college teaching career came to an end.

When I quit working, I had lost the feeling of being useful. When you don't have a routine the days just slowly go by. A friend of mine told me about PCs for People here in Mankato. It's a charity that takes in donated computers, fixes them up, and gives them out to people with low incomes. I went to the first orientation and started volunteering there right after that. I love it—my life would be much duller without it. Now I do the orientation.

On the anniversary of my daughter's death, I buy flowers and keep them at home. On her birthday, I take flowers up to the Children's Memorial and I leave them there. So, I have some things that I do. They help. I cry, but I feel better because I don't want her forgotten. A lot of people don't want to talk about it, like my family, because they think it's going to hurt me. I like to talk about her.

I think you have to find a place where you belong. It might be a place inside you, but it might be a physical place. I have both with the Wagon Wheel. It's very comfortable here.

Joel "Augie" Nickel

I feel at home here. I feel like a part of a small family, I guess. I like the small-town restaurant kind of thing—where you walk in and they know who you are.

I'd say I'm a person of caring. I care a lot about helping the other person out if you can. I can pretty much pick up a conversation with anybody. I'm community-friendly I guess. I'm also hard-working.

I've been unemployed now for about seven months. I worked at Snyder's drug store downtown for 30 years until they sold out to Walgreens. I wasn't part of the picture.

They say everything happens for a reason, I guess. Anytime you talk to these big corporate guys, they say, "Yeah, it may be hairy for a while, but in the long run it's going to be better." I believe that to a point, but then I hate to see the hometown guy out on the street, too. Here he built his business up and he's trying to put food on the table for his family and you get a corporate guy that comes in and you might just become a number to them instead of a name.

The economy is not better. I don't know when it's going get better. I don't think it's all Obama's fault. I'm not the politician type. I let them guys run the country the best they can, I guess. If you want me to vote for you, I got one thing to tell you: Don't call during a Twins or Vikings game. If you interrupt a Vikings or Twins game, you're not going to get my vote. It's plain and simple. You can call and ask for my opinion during Oprah or something like that. Then I'll give it to you.

I collect bobbleheads. Kevin got me started on that. I've got about four or five shelves in my basement. They're all lined up along there. When the Twins did Kirby Puckett, I was in line at 3:30 in the morning at the Metrodome. Some of the bobbleheads are worth real money. Harmon Killebrew is going for between two and three hundred, but I won't sell mine. My nieces are going to end up selling them all for five dollars apiece while I'm rolling over in my grave.

I'm looking for work. I got a couple prospects out there, but it's slim pickin' right now. Kevin has been really good to me during all this. I'll come in at 3:30 in the afternoon and if there are some dishes to be done, I'll help out. I figure if I didn't have Kevin and his crew down here I'd probably be sitting at home looking at four walls all day. You can't do that.

"Though a radically different kind of setting from the home, the third place is remarkably similar to a good home in the psychological comfort and support that it extends."

Ray Oldenburg—*The Great Good Place*

Kenneth Hardt

I've lived in Illinois now for many years, but I'm a Minnesotan at heart. When I return to Mankato, I'm looking at the same town but nothing is the same. It's like looking at a photograph and watching it fade from color to black and white. But the Wagon Wheel, the Wagon Wheel is still in color.

When I was maybe seven or eight, my mother was washing dishes and this guy came on the radio and used the word "Socrates." I had no idea who Socrates was so I asked my mother. She took me down to the Martin County Library in Fairmont, and that's when I got interested in history. I started reading history at such a young age that it's just part of the way I think.

I grew up during the second World War and was identified as a German. I was called a dirty little Nazi at a young age. I didn't even know what a Nazi was. It could have been a nut off a tree for all I knew, but I thought well, gee, that must be what I am. Later I learned what a Nazi was and I knew I wasn't one of them, but because of circumstance then, I had ended up identifying myself with only my father's side of the family, with only my German heritage. And so you might say when I grew up I only knew half of myself.

As I got older, I felt I had to get a balance, get a more complete picture of who I am, so I started to learn more about my mother's side of the family. They were French Canadian and were involved in the fur trade, mainly as interpreters. This is going way back—1600s, 1700s, 1800s. They learned various Indian dialects—Dakota, Lakota, Algonquin, Iroquois, along with French and in later years English. They also intermarried with Native Americans.

There is this story of a French trapper who was trapping near what is now Mankato. About the time he was trapping here, some white men looted a Dakota village while the men were gone. When the Dakota men came back, they took pursuit of the looters. They captured this French trapper and were going to kill him. The women of the village told the men that the person they captured was not among those who damaged their village, so the Dakota men let him go. This event took place right near what is now Land of Memories Park—and that French trapper was an ancestor of mine. Had the story gone another way, I wouldn't be sitting here today. This story is one reason I return to Mankato every year to attend the Pow Wow.

When I go to the Pow Wow, I don't go out there as a wannabe Indian or something. I don't go there and then run home to do bead work and say, "Oh, I'm Native American." I am what I am. But learning about others and connecting to both sides of my family's history has helped me develop different aspects of myself. I feel much more balanced because I know about who I am.

The Wagon Wheel is a piece of Mankato history that should be preserved. I hope it's around for a long time. I hope it passes on to another generation in their family. Walking in here just feels like coming home.

Ruth Spore

I used to come to the Wagon Wheel years ago after dancing at the ballroom with my husband or after one of the clubs—the VFW or American Legion. No matter the time, he always wanted to come in and have eggs.

I hadn't been in the Wagon Wheel for a few years, and then I got started with my water aerobics group from the YMCA. There are about six to thirteen of us that come in here for lunch every Monday after aerobics. It's a standing thing. They have a table set up for us every week and they know us by name.

I retired in 2000. I used to run the snack bar at Mankato West High School. I loved the kids. I didn't have any problem with them. I tried to learn their names, which they liked, and I said *please* and *thank you*. I treated them with respect. If they started swearing, I'd say, "Get to the end of the line." That was it. They respected me for it. The older kids in line would say, "You don't do that in front of her."

Sometimes I'll be walking in a store around town and a gal will come up to me and say, "You were at West when I was there…" So they still recognize me and it's nice that they do. It makes me feel good.

I started doing water aerobics at the YMCA shortly after I retired, about 11 years ago. It's very good exercise, and I really enjoy the companionship of the ladies. The group is my sounding board sometimes, especially Delores and Elaine, who have been my lifeline at times. A lot of us in the group are widows.

My husband passed away thirty years ago after an over-four-year battle with cancer. I was 44. I had a 12-year-old still at home and three other children not yet married.

Why didn't I remarry? I just didn't find anybody. I guess maybe I'm too independent. Even now my daughter will say, "Mom, you should do this or that," and it goes in one ear and out the other. I make up my own mind. I have no regrets about not meeting someone. It just wasn't meant to be.

I'm a sewer. Sewing relaxes me. I do quilts, table runners, table toppers, placemats, even book covers. I have ten grandchildren, and I've given each of them two baby quilts. I also sew quilt tops for church. Our quilts from the church group go to Lutheran World Relief, the Salvation Army, and then to countries experiencing war and third world countries. I feel very fortunate I can help in this way.

One of the waitresses here, Rebel, asked me the other day if I do embroidery. I said *ya* and she proceeded to tell me she had just become a grandmother and "bit off a little more than she could chew" by purchasing the materials to make a quilt for her new grandson. Would I maybe do it for her? So I guess I'll be making another baby quilt. That will be fun.

Elaine Harkins

You know, I've never been interviewed and you don't know how nervous I am about this [laughter]. I just kind of got roped in. Everybody in our group was sitting there that day you passed around the sign-up sheet, and nobody was signing the paper and I thought, "Somebody's got to do this."

After water aerobics we have to go out for lunch for sure. And so all at once we decided, Wagon Wheel on Mondays, and everybody loves coming here. They treat us very well here. They know us by name. They always have the table set up for us, and they practically know what we order every time.

I started water aerobics after my husband passed away. That was 18 years ago. It's good for me. It's kind of a social life for me, and it gets me out and about. Being part of a group like ours keeps your mind going. It's a good bunch. I really feel we rely on each other. You don't just sit home and get depressed.

I think it's important to be involved with things in your community. I try to get to church every Sunday and Bible Study on Thursdays. I volunteered at the Lutheran home for 14 years. I worked the front desk, greeting people and guiding their way. I've never been a real leader or anything, and I don't want to be a leader. I've always been kind of in the background. I'm comfortable there.

I grew up around Vernon Center, Minnesota—just outside of Mankato. I was lacking two months of being 19 when I got married. We were high school sweethearts. He got his draft notice and five days later we were married. My mother and sister came to town and looked for a wedding dress, and my soon-to-be husband Milan and I looked for flowers and a photographer. We sent out wedding announcements afterwards and he took off for service, first to basic training and then to Korea.

When my husband was in Korea, I stayed with my folks and worked both as a housekeeper for a lady who lived near us and as a secretary at the high school in Garden City where I graduated from. I didn't drive at that time, so would you believe I rode the school bus each day to my secretary job?

He came back home, he found a job and we settled in. Our children were born in '56, '57, '59, '61, and '64. When the kids were young I wanted to be home with them, so I took in some ironing work—station wagons full of clothes to be pressed. I also did some baking for a family.

Eventually I went back to night school and improved my typing and things so I could work outside the home. I worked in the Human Resources Department for Green Giant for ten years, and I was a receptionist with ADC for another ten years. I quit working to care for my husband. He fought cancer for six years.

Milan was 62 when he died. I was 60. You lay awake at night and worry, but it gets better over time. It's always there in the back of your mind, I guess. You have to learn to handle things, maybe. I never had to even fill the gas tank before my husband passed away. Then I had to do everything from worry about an oil change to taking care of the yard and shoveling snow. I'm glad so far I've been able to take care of myself and not have to depend on anyone.

I don't feel I'm just sitting at home in a rocking chair passing my time away. I'm 78 now—good heavens, I'm glad I'm still here.

Dolores Vaubel

Many, many years ago I would come to the Wagon Wheel after dances at the Kato Ballroom. It's an old place, and I'm an old lady [laughs].

I'm part of the water aerobics group from the YMCA that comes to the Wagon Wheel for lunch every Monday after our class. We sit here and, just like they say, chew the fat.

I raised nine children. They gave me little problems once in a while, but they all turned out wonderful. I wouldn't trade a one of them. A lot of times we'd take a Sunday drive to go look at the snowbanks [laughs]. We had a station wagon.

My five boys can do anything. I mean plumbing and carpenter work and electrical work—all of it. My daughters can't necessarily do all that, but they can do all kinds of other things. One of them is a seamstress, one of them works at a school, one of them works at Mankato Clinic, and one of them does beautiful ceramic work. My kids can all do a lot of things.

After my youngest daughter started first grade, I went and cleaned houses for other people. I could set my own hours, so I was always home when my children left for school, and I always got home before they got home. I've heard people say, "Cleaning houses ain't much of a job." Well, you know what, it was. I felt good about myself. You satisfied those other people and they liked your work. I knew I accomplished something.

My husband passed away in 1991. He was 65. Truthfully, I do not know what was wrong with him. His body got so that it did not work. His arms did not work, his legs did not work, and his brain did not work right anymore. He went to Rochester and had bypass, but it didn't do him one bit of good. It was discouraging to watch because he had been such an active man. It went on for four or five years.

I had started going to the YMCA before he died, and I got even more involved after.

The YMCA and the water aerobics group there play a real important role in my life. I'm there every day. I think life would be very boring without the Y. It's important to have a community and friends. Otherwise, I would sit home day after day and probably get depressed from sitting home.

After my husband passed away, I started volunteering around the community. I worked at a thrift store that donated its profits to help the handicapped, and I still volunteer at my church setting up tables for lunches after funerals. I also tie knots for quilts that our church donates to places like the Salvation Army and a shelter for battered women. Doing these things has helped make me more outgoing than I used to be. I used to be more quiet.

At 83, I have more aches and pains than I used to, but it doesn't do any good to complain about them. Dying doesn't scare me. When it's my time, I'm ready to go. Whenever somebody dies, I always tell the kids I'm next on the list, and they say, "Mom, don't say that." But I don't go, so I guess I'm not ready yet.

During our lunches at the Wagon Wheel, sometimes somebody will have a picture of their grandkids and they'll bring that and pass it around, or sometimes we'll talk about who came to your house to visit, you know. We just talk about life in general, I guess. I enjoy our time together.

"In order for the city
and its neighborhoods
to offer the rich and varied association
that is their promise and potential,
there must be neutral ground upon which
people may gather. There must be places
where individuals may come and go as
they please, in which no one
is required to play host, and in which we
all feel at home and comfortable."

Ray Oldenburg—*The Great Good Place*

John Harrington

Every walk of life is in the Wagon Wheel, from the person who has absolutely nothing to the person who can buy the town. You don't feel like you have to bow down to the guy with all the money, and nobody looks down on the guy without money. Everybody's equal when you walk in here. That's kind of a neat feeling.

I went to St. Mary's University in Winona, played one year of basketball there, blew my knee out, and came back to Mankato. I spent the next 12 years coaching at my alma mater, Loyola High School. I coached in the winter and worked construction in the summer. I really enjoyed it.

Later in life I went back to college and got a teaching degree. After earning my degree, I taught and coached for two years at another school. Last one hired, first one let go. I then applied for the head coaching position at Loyola, and I didn't get it. That hurt. I'd dedicated 12 years to coaching there, went to school there, and played basketball there. I was really hurting and feeling bad about it. Then the radio thing fell into place.

One day I was at a Loyola basketball game and the local radio announcer, who I knew, called me over and asked me to talk on air about how I thought Loyola would be that year—as a pregame. So I did. That was 23 years ago and now they can't get me off the air. I do color commentary and a little play-by-play for a lot of local teams—Loyola, Mankato East and West, Bethany, and some MSU, to name a few.

To do radio, you have to stay involved with the game. You really get to know the coaches and players—who they are and what they're all about. You become part of the game instead of being just a casual fan. It's like coaching in a way. I like that.

My "real job" is in sales for JRM Promotions here in town; we do the Wagon Wheel mugs and shirts among other things. I enjoy sales, but doing radio makes me feel especially good because you're making other people feel good. Radio ties the community together. I get comments all the time saying it's so great you talk about my son or grandson. I'm glad I can do that for people.

There aren't many restaurants you go into where the owner yells at you when you come in the door. "No bouncer today? Who let you in?" No offense to the chains, but it's not the same feeling. It's kind of more of a factory-in-and-out type feeling with the chains. You never feel like that at the Wagon Wheel.

Harry B. Coonce

I've been coming to the Wagon Wheel since about 1970. It's always good to talk to Kevin. He's a Twins fan, of course, and I've been a Cardinal fan all my life, so sometimes I put my Cardinal cap up on a stand or wherever and just wait for him to notice it.

I guess since I was four years old and first taken to pre-kindergarten, I always liked going to school. I mean, what a great deal. You just sit there and people will tell you things and you can just soak it up. I soak up things pretty well.

I taught college mathematics for forty-some years. I retired in 1999. I taught at 13 or 14 different schools and lived in 19 different states. I went from Undergraduate Teaching Assistant to Graduate Teaching Assistant to Lecturer to Assistant Professor, Associate Professor, Full Professor and Professor Emeritus. You know what comes next? Dead professor.

Mathematics is not about making a faster car or a rocket ship or even solving a financial crisis. All this crap you see on TV about "do the math," they're talking about arithmetic, not mathematics. Mathematics is an art. Any mathematician worthy of the title has some set of theorems he or she has proven. These theorems tell us something about the world that was not known before the mathematician proved them. Mathematics is a quest for knowledge.

Each week in my introductory mathematics class, we would talk about a different theorem. Take the Pythagorean theorem, for example—a theorem everybody has probably heard of, proven in the sixth century B.C. by Pythagoras. On Monday we'd prove it one way, on Tuesday I'd given them an entirely different proof, and on Wednesday we'd have another. I told them that on the quiz they would have to tell me which proof they thought was the prettiest and which one they liked the best. I told them they would receive a zero if they put down they liked a proof best because it was the easiest.

Back in the mid-1990s, I started what is called the Mathematics Genealogy Project. It's a database available online for every professional mathematician. There are about 158,000 people in the project now. I wanted to trace intellectual history from way back, to find out where mathematicians got their degrees, who their advisors were, what their thesis was about, what theorems they were working on—those sorts of things. I worked on the project almost every day from 1995 until 2008, when I passed it off to others.

Teaching got more difficult in the 1990s. It was a bad decade. Students in my classes were always asking, "How am I going to use this?" I don't care how you're going to use this. I'm trying to teach you something about what we know. How you use this is up to you.

Education is about understanding what things are—history, literature, mathematics. To become educated is to try to learn as much as you can about what our civilization has created over several thousand years. Training is teaching someone to put this nut onto this bolt. I refused to teach like a trainer. I wouldn't do it.

The Wagon Wheel is a place where I'm comfortable. You see some people that you suspect may have a different station in life or maybe they're struggling, and you see some of the wealthiest guys in town come in here, too. It's a fine institution, this place.

Laurel Garvin

The Wagon Wheel is kind of like a grounding place. I sit and read the paper, drink some coffee, chat with some people, and I just kind of revive.

What has being a single parent taught me? Good question. I learned I can handle a lot more than I thought I could. I learned that the human spirit is so immensely strong, and that we don't give it enough credit. I learned there's never enough money, there's never enough time, and there's never enough patience. Being a single parent is challenging at times, but it's amazing and rewarding too.

My husband Brian and I were married for ten years. We were kind of like a comedy team together. We were both what I would term adult Peter Pans—neither of us wanted to grow up all the way. It was a good time. We had two little boys together, Weston and Taylor.

Brian passed away in 1998 after a four-year battle with heart disease. He was 40. Weston was nine when Brian died, and Taylor was three.

Brian was in radio and known all over the place around here. The funeral was huge. The first time I felt, truly, just fear in the pit of my stomach was when we were coming down the Main Street hill behind the hearse carrying my husband to the cemetery. I looked back and there was this nonstop string of cars following us. It was like, "Oh my God, this is really happening."

The people at the Wagon Wheel are part of the community that has helped me raise my boys. They hear stories about their dad here. Both of the boys played football growing up, and Kevin and others down here would visit with them about the games and whatnot. More often than not, someone will still say to one of them, "Are you Brian Garvin's son?" These kinds of things are very important for boys growing up without a male influence in their lives.

I've always been musical. I've played the piano for years. I taught myself how to play the guitar, and one of these days I'm going to take lessons and learn how to do it for real. I'm also a writer. I have about four books going—one of them is about my parents, and one is about my trip to Europe while I was in college.

At 53, it gets a little scary moving forward with the boys all grown, you know, but I have no regrets. There's nothing I treasure more than sitting around our backyard, making S'mores, sharing stories with friends, and sharing my sons with friends. I know my boys are going to have incredibly great childhood memories, and that's what it's all about. That's what my parents gave me and what I want to give Weston and Taylor.

They say God only gives you as much as you can handle. Sometimes I think He respects me way too much. But overall I've always been a real happy and hopeful person, and the Wagon Wheel is one of the things that makes me happy.

Harlan Mehlhop

Do I like change? Yeah I like change, but I don't like all changes. I feel our society is losing some of its cohesiveness and its willingness to work together. But at the Wagon Wheel they haven't lost that yet. Coming in here lets me hold on to that feeling of cohesiveness a little bit longer.

I married after the service. Had three children. Then my wife passed away. My first marriage was wonderful. Wonderful children and now wonderful grandchildren. As much as I loved her and as much as I miss her, I still felt the need to have a relationship again.

I'm German Lutheran and my faith is my number one thought. I believe I will reach the heavens because, although I have sinned, by the grace of God I will be forgiven. My faith helps me withstand the setbacks I have had in life and to think of them in a good way, to spin it that I wasn't being punished for something. I was just being tested. I believe we're all being tested every day.

Sometime after my first wife passed away, my pastor said, "Well, if you decide to get married again, let me know." One day I came back and said, "You know, Pastor, I found a lady that I like, but she's Irish Catholic." My pastor told me that was ok—"just see how it works out."

Marcia and I were married ten years ago. Our wedding was held at her church in rural Madison Lake, Marysburg Catholic Church. But I wanted my church to recognize the union as well. So right when we got done with the wedding in her church, we drove to my Lutheran church in New Ulm and had our wedding vows blessed.

After the blessing of our marriage in my church, we drove to the Country Club in New Ulm for our reception. We had the German flag and the Irish flag crossed at the head table. We had Irish beer and German wine. And we had a band that played every other song German, then Irish. Today we're one big happy Irish/German family. Let me put it another way: We're one big GERMAN/Irish family [laughs].

Eagles are my favorite bird for a number of reasons—two of them being that eagles are a symbol for the strength of our country and that they are mentioned in Isaiah in the Bible. I collect Kennedy eagle half dollars, and I have lots of eagles in my house. I like that eagles were almost extinct, but that we can now watch them soar over our Lake Washington.

You see a lot of different people in the Wagon Wheel—young and old, they are all here. So you come in. It's just a sense of feeling good about yourself, and feeling that they appreciate you being here.

"Within third places,
the charm and flavor of one's personality,
irrespective of his or her station in life,
is what counts."

Ray Oldenburg—*The Great Good Place*

Ted & Cortnee Wilcox

Editor's Note – Cortnee Wilcox's comments are in italics.

Coming to the Wagon Wheel is like jumping into an old-time magazine and sitting in it. It's so different from everything else. I like that it's cheap, too. That's good for a college student.

The Wagon Wheel is our conversation point. We try to get here once a week, usually for breakfast. This place crosses generations very easily, that's one reason we come—and it just feels like a family setting.

Sometimes I'll get to breakfast before him and the waitress will say, "Is grandpa coming today?" "Yup, he's coming," I'll say, and then they'll put out the two menus on the table and pour his coffee before he even gets in the door.

I had three kids and was married and divorced by the time I was 23. My ex-wife went to Colorado with the kids when they were fairly young, so I didn't have the chance to be the kind of father figure I should have been to my kids.

I really don't have a close relationship with my father. He lives far away and never had anything to do with my life. Grandpa has always been the one that I can talk to about anything. He became a grandpa at 37, so he's always seemed like a dad.

I see my relationship with Cortnee, and with all of my grandchildren, as a second chance to help raise children. I really missed out on the family thing, and it was a need I had. I'm especially close to Cortnee because she's here in town and she was the first.

I've been a student at Minnesota State University for five years now. I'm going to be an elementary or middle school teacher. I've always connected with kids. I really love watching a child's eyes light up when you help them with something, and all of the sudden they're like, "Oh, I get it." There's no other feeling that can compare to that.

She's also a great singer. She started singing at a little bar and grill down in Truman, Minnesota, when she was about ten. She sings mostly country music. She's won a bunch of local radio contests and performed twice for 11,000 people in the grandstand at the State Fair during the talent contest. Watching her sing is awesome. I'm so proud watching her that I have a hard time keeping the buttons from popping off my chest.

When I was little it felt like grandpa and I went to the park every day. I remember the tire swing and the merry-go-round. Then in the evenings we'd go out to eat and I'd have a grilled cheese and chips every time.

Divorce isn't fun. It has all kinds of issues and complications. I hope in some way I'm making amends by having the kind of relationship with Cortnee and my other grandchildren that I would have tried to have with my children. Like I said, it's a second chance.

I'm getting married in a few months. Grandpa and my other grandpa from Colorado are going to walk me down the aisle.

What a deal, huh? What a deal.

Randy Wells

The Wagon Wheel is my second home in the morning. I'm here five days a week. The waitresses here know every one of us, and they'll joke with us a little bit. I like that.

I moved here in 1968 at the age of 32. I always wanted to go to college, so I came down here and went to MSU, Mankato. I have a degree in Industrial Technical Studies, which is a fancy way of saying industrial arts.

I planned to become a teacher, but after student teaching I decided that at my age I wasn't willing to be a teacher. I expected the students to want to learn and not to have to force-feed them. I also expected them to have more discipline.

After getting my degree, I picked up my hammer and went to work on my own. I've owned my own construction business since January 1971. We build post frame buildings for people who have a lot of toys like 4-wheelers, boats, and motor homes. We don't build cheap buildings, our buildings are high-quality from one end to the other. We do some home remolding and shingling, too. I have a list of 240 customers that we've had over the years.

If you want to get ahead today, regardless of what you do, you better have a good work ethic. I get a little critical of myself, because I'm just about 75 years old and my work ethic isn't what it used to be. I can't get out of bed as early in the morning, and I wear out quicker at the end of the day, but I still think it's important to get things done.

What am I proudest of? That's a good question. I'm definitely proudest of the kids, there's no doubt about it. I'm also proud of the business and that I don't have to go out and stand on the street corner for my next meal. My wife Beth and I have been married 50 years, and that's an accomplishment. She's to be rewarded for that, too, because I'm not the easiest person in the world to live with. You can put that in the story because that's very true.

About 30 years ago, my wife and I got into the Hackney show pony business. We raise the ponies and show them in shows around the country. They're little horses. They go from about 48 inches at the shoulder to 54 at the shoulder. They have huge engines in them, huge hearts. They just got a lot of zip. If I'm having a tough day, I can go outside and watch the mares and colts run, and I have a better day just from doing that.

I think kids should learn to work with their hands. They should learn to make things. We need industrial arts back in grade school, maybe as early as the first grade. I know the computer has taken over a lot, but we still need our hands to build things, and a lot of satisfaction comes from that. And if kids learned to fix things, do some of their own plumbing or whatever, they'd save themselves a lot of money when they got older.

I like coming to the Wagon Wheel because it's on my level. I can dress in a tux, but it's still me inside it. I come down here, and I can put on my overalls and be comfortable. We'd be better off if we had more of these kinds of places.

Royal Lee

The Bullshippers coffee group has been going for thirty years or more. I'm the only surviving member of the original group, and I'm the oldest. I'm 93. I'm the king [laughs].

I went into the Army on February 10th of 1941—about 11 months before Pearl Harbor. I was captured by the Germans on the 17th of February, 1943. I escaped in May of 1945.

We were in North Africa and found ourselves way outnumbered. There were eleven battalions of German infantry, and we were sitting out there with one regiment of tanks and two battalions of infantry. We realized we just couldn't circle back so we decided to hide in some cactus patches until dark.

This local found us in the cactus patch. "You're surrounded," he said. "You stay here, and I'll come back when it gets dark and help you get out." This should have made us think a little bit, but it sounded good [chuckles]. He left and was gone probably 45 minutes or an hour, and we heard some mechanized units running past where we were. We looked out, and here's this guy we just talked with riding in a German armored car, and he's pointing out where we are and they start firing in there.

You just hoped, you know. You just existed, that's all. You did make some very, very good close friends. There were about 1500 of us in the camp, and you were with one another all the time, day and night. There was a mess hall and we were assigned a table. There were eight men at a table, and every day when we'd come in, there'd be a loaf of German black bread on the table. We'd take turns slicing that into eight pieces, and the guy that sliced it got last choice. After cutting, you worked your way back up—you got a better choice each day.

In January of '45, the Russians had started their drive, so we had to be moved. They told us we'd walk and catch the train. And we went 235 miles. On foot. At night we'd stay in barns or sheds. Some of the barns had hay in them, and guys would lie in the hay and some of them would burrow down in the hay. Well, the next morning, why, the Germans would count—and if the count didn't come out, they would go up there with their submachine guns and spray the hay.

I finally wound up in Stalag 3A, which was Southwest of Berlin about 15–20 miles. One day, two friends of mine and I were walking along there, and we got to a place where we could get through the fences. There were two barbwire fences, and they were three or four feet apart. In between there was just a maze of barbwire. We got through that and ran to an American patrol.

The Wagon Wheel puts up with us—let's put it that way. You become very friendly with the coffee group. You consider them among your best friends. Sometimes a stranger will come into the group, sit down, and just melt right in with the rest of us. We know all the answers, but nobody listens.

Erv Kurth

I'm one of the younger people in the Bullshippers coffee club down at the Wagon Wheel—I'm only 90. We meet at 9:30 Monday through Friday to resolve the questions of the day. Some days I come home with words of wisdom, other days I have difficulty interpreting what I heard [laughs].

Members of the Bullshippers come from all walks of life, and our conversation covers a wide range of topics, including religion. It always amazes me how religious topics can be discussed, and no one becomes too irritated or concerned with what is being said.

Our group celebrates birthdays, and the honored buys the coffee and cookies that day—for this, we sing happy birthday. If John Berg and Kelly Gage are there, it sounds pretty good. Other days it may be a little weak. We do a little bit of gambling, too, just to make sure that everybody is still financially sound.

Since 2002, I've technically been retired. I spent my career in banking. What I always liked about banking was meeting the people. You met a diverse group of people, and it was a pleasure if you could give them some help. One of my biggest joys was helping somebody buy a house. I derived the most pleasure out of helping older people who had striven very hard for a number of years to get a small amount of money assembled so they could make a down payment.

For entertainment or self-preservation, I take an active role in church, golf, the Wagon Wheel, and curling.

I started curling in January of 1958 and never stopped. I think I'd been working in the bank maybe two weeks, and a friend came in and said, "You are now going to be a member of the curling club, give me a hundred dollars." And so, I was a member of the curling club [laughs]. I'm the oldest active member of the club. The people who curl tend to have the ability to laugh at themselves, and I like that. I think that's also true of the crew at the Wagon Wheel.

My wife and I met in Montana, and we were married there in 1954. We lived in Billings, Montana, and Dickinson, North Dakota, before moving to Mankato in 1957. She passed away about 22 years ago. Let's say when you lose someone you've lived with for a long time, it leaves a big hole, and that hole never is completely filled. I had a book given to me by my pastor that helped me understand what was going on in my mind and body after my wife passed away. It encouraged me to try and resume a normal life, even though initially it feels you're only half a life.

I don't really have any words of wisdom. I feel very fortunate. I've had relatively minor health problems over the years, and I have great friends and family. I do think God blesses us in various ways, and I think in my case maybe He feels I'm not strong enough to take the tough burden. He gives me an easier one.

"The persistent mood of the third place
is a playful one…
Every topic and speaker
is a playful trapeze
for the exercise and display of wit."

Ray Oldenburg—*The Great Good Place*

Paul Meyer

Editor's Note – Doris Meyer's comments are in italics.

The Wagon Wheel is just a warm place to go. It's like an old shoe. I meet down there with a coffee group that calls itself the Bullshippers. We're a very diverse group. We've got a retired doctor, retired school teachers, a retired banker, a retired investment individual, and a retired dentist, to name a few. I enjoy listening to all the yack, yack, yack and trying to figure out what they said.

I was born on the 18th day of May of 1918—that makes me 92 years old. Even at 92 you can still do things, and people accept you as being 92. They don't expect too much of you. I look around the congregation, and I'm the oldest one there, but that doesn't bother me any.

My first wife, Wilda, died from cancer. That's the low spot in my life. But that happens—everybody has happy times and sad times. We were married 45 years.

Doris and I met in a rather unique way. I was at church one day, and I saw this man sitting back there by himself. My first wife was at the hospital having an operation, so I was alone at church and went back to visit with this man. I walked up and I said, "I see you're here alone too. My name is Meyer, M-E-Y-E-R." He stood up and said, "Well, my name is Beyer, B-E-Y-E-R." I found out that his wife Doris was in the same hospital as my wife. The four of us visited later at the hospital and made a connection. From that time on the two couples just bonded. The four of us did a lot of things together.

His wife passed away the same year that my husband passed away. Paul and I started going out for meals and drives. Most of the time he'd talk about things he and Wilda did during their marriage, and I'd talk about my husband, whose name also happened to be Paul. So it started out just sharing thoughts of our marriages, and that was real good for us—to get over the grief in that way. We never thought about it as a date.

One day we met friends at a restaurant, and they looked at us and said, "You two look like you want to get married." Then we were at T.G.I. Friday's one day having noon lunch, and the waitress came up and said, "You two look like lovebirds." So I guess we started thinking maybe there is something here.

I was sitting on a chair in my apartment—it must have been after we had dinner. He got down on his knee and said, "Will you marry me?" I said yes.

It was just one of those things that are made in heaven. We both had been happy in our marriages, we both lost our spouses, and we had a good fit to know each other. We saw more and more of each other and finally decided: Why not get a better income tax [joint laughter]?

I'm sure glad the coffee group exists. It's wonderful for these fellows to get together—the camaraderie and having each other for support. They're just bullshippers.

Frank Brown

I've discovered that everybody has a sense of spirituality, whether or not you identify with a specific denomination or religious group. We all have a spiritual nature that connects us with something greater than ourselves.

I moved to Mankato about 12 years ago after retiring as a hospital chaplain, serving first at Mayo Clinic and then at Kansas City Research Medical Center. Prior to being a hospital chaplain, I had been a Presbyterian pastor for 25 years in North Carolina, Virginia, and Florida.

When I got to Mankato, I was invited to join the Bullshippers, a coffee group down at the Wagon Wheel. The group has such a mix of people, and it has been a real privilege for me to get to know a whole cross section of Mankato. I'm kind of the informal chaplain for the Bullshippers, just as our dentist gives us advice sometimes, and our physician, too.

When people find out I was a hospital chaplain, they sometimes ask, "Wasn't that depressing to visit with sick people all the time?" But it wasn't depressing. It was really very gratifying to know that I had the privilege of walking into a patient's room and having them share with me their concerns. Illness is a very isolating and lonely experience, and part of my role was to enter a patient's life and help bring them out of their loneliness into contact with their spirituality and their community.

The experiences with children were the most difficult. To see what those families, those beautiful families had to go through was draining. Part of my job was just being a friend to the child, maybe playing a game with whatever toys might be on the bed. But another responsibility was to the parents, who were just going through hell.

Families would often ask, "Why, God? Why does this happen to us?" The only answer I can give, and it's not really an answer, is to say that it's not fair, it's just not fair.

My relationship with my wife came about through my chaplaincy. Her son John John was in a motorcycle accident here in Mankato. They brought him to Methodist Hospital in Rochester. I followed John John for about two weeks until he died. His mother and I became acquainted through this tragedy, and we were married seven years later. I've always said that the good thing that came out of John John's death was that he brought Dee and me together. And that's helped, I think, in her grief and with my grief, too.

The kind of God I serve and worship is a God that does not manipulate and tell me exactly what I should do, but a God who gives me freedom of choice. I believe in a God who suffers and rejoices with me.

I find a fellowship with the Bullshippers that exists nowhere else in my life. There's a support group there that helps me to see that there are good people in the world. In some ways it is a spiritual group. I can share my human thoughts with the group and feel acceptance. The Bullshippers turned out to be one of my salvations.

Bob Browne

The guys in the Bullshippers engage in a lot of good-natured razzing of one another. I occasionally get picked on for the size of my ears: "How can you be hard of hearing with ears so big?" someone will say. I deserve anything I ever get.

I have lived in Mankato most of my life, with the exception of two years working with the Continental Can Company in St. Louis and Chicago, and two years of military service during the Korean War.

They estimate over 4,000 rounds of artillery pounded us the night I was wounded a second time in Korea. It's indescribable. It is just a constant, terribly loud blast, you know, like you live next to a quarry or something, and the noise is just compounded hundreds of times over because they just keep blitzing the same patch of ground. When it was over, you would swear that you were the only one left alive. I think we only had one or two dead and five or six wounded. I was left with a severe concussion and have headaches to this day.

I never believed in any of that stuff about Post-Traumatic Stress Disorder before I experienced it. Maybe that's why the old boy upstairs bumped me through it.

There are several aspects of Post-Traumatic Stress Disorder. I could be sitting here talking with you, and all of a sudden tears will start flowing, for no reason that I know of—that is the most annoying and embarrassing part. You never relax, you're never at ease. One night about five years ago, my wife Sue woke me up. I'd grabbed the calf of her leg while I was sleeping. A day later you could see where every finger and my thumb had squeezed that leg.

Ever since shortly after the war until just a couple years before I retired, my doctor would take x-rays of my head searching for the cause of my headaches. When we got the new CT scanner in town, he called me in so he could do a scan instead of an old-fashioned X-ray. "Bob, we found brain damage," he said. "Damn you, Doc," I said, "You call me in and use all that expensive equipment, pile it all up on the taxpayers, when anyone in town could have told you I have brain damage."

Turns out I've got massive blood clots from the concussion I suffered 60 years ago in Korea. He said we either have to pull out the blood clots, which could kill you, or we can leave them in, but you'll probably die from them. You'll get jarred in an auto accident, or a couple of them will move just from your being overly active, and that will kill you. I didn't have them taken out. I don't know why, but I just dismiss those things. A guy could step off the curb and get hit by a car and he's all done, you know.

Post Traumatic Stress Disorder and the headaches have been with me pretty much constantly since immediately after the war. After a while, though, you go back to your old routines, which for me was being the village idiot. Through therapy and with the help of others, I am fortunate enough to be living a happy life. I live in a wonderful part of a wonderful country. I have a beautiful family and had a long career in business. I have no regrets at all about serving my country.

John Marso

I'm a newcomer to the Bullhshippers coffee group down here at the Wagon Wheel. I've only been a part of this organization for about four years. I think I'm still being evaluated [laughs]. Maybe they won't even keep me.

It's a fun group. You have a cup of coffee and you shoot the bull. Your status in life doesn't matter in the group. If you're a billionaire, you're still Joe Blow, but you have to be a pretty good bullshipper to keep up with these guys. The name of the group is very apropos.

My dad and mother were both born in the late 1800s. I don't think my mother went past the eighth grade. My dad was a high school graduate, I know that. He was from South Dakota and he was in the clothing business. He told me one time he was the salutatorian of his class in high school, and that that meant he was second in his class. "Really," I said, "how many were in your class?" "Three," he said.

I graduated from high school here in Mankato back a little bit before Christ. I had a scholarship to the University of Minnesota to play football, but I wasn't really excited about it, so I went to St. Thomas, a far smaller school, also on a football scholarship. After my first year in college, I got drafted and shipped to Korea for two years. When I returned home, I finished my degree and went on to medical school.

I practiced medicine for 30 years here in Mankato. I was an OB/GYN—delivering babies, doing female surgery and that type of thing. I kept a reasonable tab of the number of babies I delivered over the years. It was a little over 10,000, something like 10,200. It was a very rewarding practice, obviously.

When I was practicing, your patients got to know you and you got to know them. You typically don't have that intimate relationship anymore now that people go to a clinic or an emergency room and see Dr. X or Dr. Y. Of course, the closer relationships meant you were always on call and always had to be on the ball: weekends, weekdays, 52 weeks a year, seven days a week. I often put in 100-hour weeks.

I retired in 1984 at the age of 56. One of my philosophies in life is that if you can retire, retire. It's a hell of a lot better than working. I mean, wherever you're working you've got aggravations and deadlines, and if something goes wrong you've got to solve it. Retirement is a lot easier life. And if you think you have to keep working at age 70 because your experience is so great and your advice is so valuable, forget it. The younger guys are a hell of a lot better [laughing].

It always feels like old home week in the Wagon Wheel, that's what it comes down to. Right away you know about three people as you walk down the aisle. You say hello, ask them what they did yesterday or anything else. It's not a high-class place, it's a fun and casual place. You don't have to worry about anything fancy, you just play it be ear. That's my feeling on it.

"The third place is just so much space
unless the right people are there
to make it come alive,
and they are the regulars."

Ray Oldenburg—*The Great Good Place*

Jerry Hansen

I come down to the Wagon Wheel for coffee four to five times a week to meet with the Bullshippers coffee group. It's a very comfortable group to sit down and visit with. We're all from different walks of life. Some are from two or three different walks of life.

I've lived in Mankato about 12 years now. I farmed down near Delevan, Minnesota, for over 50 years. We moved to Mankato on September 9, 1999. My wife Helen picked that date for us to leave the farm because she thought that would be a kind of unique date to remember—9/9 of '99.

Up on the wall in my den, I have a toy model of every tractor I ever owned. I would guess there are about 40 of them. My dad had all International tractors, and when I came home with the first John Deere he was almost insulted. He wasn't sure if I was on the right track.

Farming was my main job, but I also had an insurance agency that I operated for 29 years. That fit in very good with the farming because most of my insurance was written to farmers. When it came to selling insurance, I just enjoyed the people. It felt like you were doing a service for those in your community. If they called you at five in the morning with a concern, you'd better be there to see them.

I had a man call me about a policy one night at 11 p.m. while I was sleeping. It was just pouring down rain, and he wanted me to come over and write him hail insurance. His corn was just coming up, so he was nervous. I went over and wrote him the policy, although we never did get any hail that night.

You have to remember that almost all people are good. I served on the school board for about 12 years, the Farmers' Elevator board for 10 years, and the insurance company board for 20 years. On some of these boards and while I was selling insurance, I realized that you're going to work with a lot of different personalities, but I just walked into all interactions with the assumption that people are good.

Helen and I have been married 58 years. We've raised two daughters and have four grandchildren. We've been square dancing for over 50 years now. You can be awfully tired when you leave home for the dance, maybe you've worked hard all day, but when you get there it's relaxing. The music perks you up a little bit and you're ready to go. It's great, even for a person with two left feet like me. I've enjoyed it immensely.

I don't think any of us guys has any special purpose when we walk into the Wagon Wheel each day. But, by the time we leave, we all come home with some new information from our fellowmen. We learn things from each other.

John Berg

The Bullshippers coffee group is really quite a bunch. We talk a little politics, a little weather, and maybe a little too much World War II. If we have a dental problem we might ask the dentist in the group, but we don't ask the minister in the group to give us too much guidance. We have a typed list of members, and right now there are about 20 active. At the bottom of the membership list are those who have passed on.

I flew B-24s in World War II. Being in the war was an important part of my life, yes, but it's one slice of the pie. It's like you have a pie and you cut it up into slices, and you lift one piece out of there that's separate from all the rest. You go to war, and then pretty soon you're out and you're back in a shirt and tie and back in school.

I thought about trying to get on with an airline after the war, but I'd had enough of flying. My favorite subjects in high school had been band and basketball. That's not very much of an academic show that I'm speaking of here. I did take some Latin. They told me I had to have it. I never have figured out why. I don't really remember ever using it. I ended up using the GI Bill to attend the University of Minnesota and study music.

After college, I directed school bands around Southern Minnesota for 38 years. My last job was at Mankato East. I was there from 1974 when the school opened until I retired in 1985. Music does something to the soul. It moves a person. It does something inside. You ever hear "Taps" played well?

As a band or choral director, there's a certain amount of control you have. It's quiet in the room and all of a sudden you bring your baton up and down and . . . *boom*, they start playing. And you started that, with just that little motion.

I like to think my students learned about more than music. Every kid in the band has an important role to play, even if they're the 17th or 18th chair. You say to the kid, "We need you here, we are counting on you." This teaches them about life and discipline, about being on time and being faithful. They have a job. Somebody else can't do all the work.

I had so many good students. I think it's important they remember you were a good band director, but also that you were a good person. That you were knowledgeable about other things too, so you could talk to them. They had interests other than music, you know. I have students who are doctors and lawyers and Ph.D.s and band directors and so forth. They see you and, if you haven't seen them for a while, they tell you "you haven't changed a bit." Now, don't you think that makes you feel young again?

I'm 88 now, and the coffee group at the Wagon Wheel is just a wonderful thing to see. We have five that are in their 90s. To see these people that active makes me feel younger. And, of course, those who are just turning 80 or 81, they see this group and think, "Look, these guys are still interested. They still talk about sports and politics and other things." It keeps you going.

Rob Foster

They say when my grandpa got off the bus after the war, his older brother picked him up to take him home and their first stop was the Wagon Wheel—to have a cup of coffee and talk about what grandpa did and saw in the war.

The Wagon Wheel is an extension of your living room. The regulars keep coming in and chatting with each other and not running out of things to say. I really like sitting in the back and hearing that table of old-timers. Everybody here has a common ground, I guess, an unspoken type of thing.

One day in here, an older guy came up to me and started talking to me about my nose ring. He asked me how my mom liked it, and I told him I was sure my mom would rather I didn't have it. Then he said something like, "My mom died when I was six years old, so you might want to make yours happy while you got her." He was just trying to give me his advice from his experience, and I value that from anybody, whether I agree or not.

I think it is important to hear people, just to give them a chance to say anything they need to say, and to really be willing to at least give it the benefit of thought.

I'm a 33-year-old single dad to a 12-year-old boy. He's with me five days a week and with his mom on the weekends. I work full-time as a tattoo artist, which I've been doing for ten years. Raising my kid, eating at the Wagon Wheel, and tattooing people is a lot of what I do right now.

I always say to myself that I have no right to complain about being a single father, because there are five million single mothers that have been doing it since the dawn of time. I do have to play both roles a lot of the time. I have to be the good cop and the bad cop, I have to cook the meals, get the homework done, do the discipline, and then get my own drawing done after he goes to bed. Being a single dad is one of the most stressful things I've ever done, but it's an amazing adventure.

My son and I are super close. He's a complete music enthusiast and a skateboarding junkie. My hopes for him? That he learns to channel his amazing amount of energy into something productive and positive. I talked with him about this just the other day. We were talking about music, and we started talking about the importance of practice. I said that if you work your butt off now at the things you love doing, you won't have to be working a job you hate when you're my age. It was kind of funny to see the little lightbulb go off in his head—it was kind of like, "Oh yeah, if I do something like that, I will get to do something like my father does, where he loves his job."

Tattoo artists are no longer always convicts and bikers. I think a real tattoo artist is someone who needs to create, and this is a great outlet for it. A tattoo artist is someone who is able to make an original piece of artwork every day on the job. How many other artists sell an original piece of artwork every day?

I have actually cried at work. Just knowing what tattoos mean to people sometimes is pretty crazy. I do not work just for the place that employees me. I work for each individual person that hires me to put something meaningful on them. I'm putting something on a person that they are going to have for the rest of their lives. I want to make sure I do it right, and that I do them justice.

The big name restaurants spend millions of dollars to market their food to you. Basically, you're being bought in that type of situation. At a place like the Wagon Wheel, you come in because you're supporting your neighbors and they're supporting you.

Dan Dinsmore & Emily Green

Editor's Note – Emily Green's comments are in italics.

For almost ten years, we kept running into one another around town. He always remembered my name. I was really impressed with that. A few years ago, we had this summer where it seemed like I ran into him every time I went downtown or to a restaurant or a party. I remember telling my sister that I just felt like somebody somewhere is trying to throw us together.

We are recently engaged. We'll be married in September 2012. Emily is very tuned in to people. She is very calm, very collected, very caring—very, very caring.

I think the Wagon Wheel is a good metaphor for our whole relationship. We both enjoy the nostalgic and the simple things. I like the retro orange booths, the individual jukeboxes, and the fact that the waitresses know everybody and know our order.

When you come to the Wagon Wheel, you are almost forced to interact with the people around you. I think people actually come down here to interact. It's kind of a step back. They don't have Wi-Fi.

He owns a photography studio down the street. He shoots weddings and graduation photos, among other things. When he was just getting started in the business, and before we knew each other, he shot my senior picture. He did a great job. I wish I had some with to show you. I look like such a girly girl in the photos, even though I wasn't much of a girly girl. I was kind of a tomboy.

I hold the creative process in a pretty high esteem. It is just a heightened sense of awareness of what is around you, whether it is a song or a painting or photography.

What I do is not all about dollars and cents. Especially in this digital age, a printed photo of a person might be the only thing that survives.

I've been a hair stylist for about four years now. I like it. You really have to be creative to be good at it. It's an art, it really is. And you feel a sense of accomplishment if your customer likes what you did. I've had people literally cry in my chair because they wanted a makeover, basically, they are at a point in their lives where they want some sort of change.

Sometimes I even get free haircuts, which is nice. She also does hair for some of my clients before a photo shoot, and does an excellent job.

I recently decided to go back to college. I'm majoring in History. Ever since I was little and my mom would read us books and tour old houses and stuff, I've loved history. There are so many cool stories about where we come from. Everyone is like, "History, what are you going to do with that?" I have no idea what I'll do—maybe work in a museum or a gallery, I don't know. All I know is I'm enjoying learning, and that it is enriching my life.

I'm very proud of her for going back to school. It is something she has always wanted to do, and one day she just said she was going to do it. She's gotten straight A's pretty much. She's really committed to it.

I think we're both a little older and wiser at this point in our lives. We just know what works. I can't really explain it, why we work so well together, but we do. He makes me laugh.

"Third places are not,
with few exceptions, advertised;
they are not elegant.
In cultures where mass advertising prevails
and appearance is valued over substance,
the third place is all the more likely
not to impress the uninitiated."

Ray Oldenburg—*The Great Good Place*

John & Kathy Dorn

Editor's Note – Kathy Dorn's comments are in italics.

We both grew up in Mankato, and in high school the Wagon Wheel was the place to go. A group of girls would go down there to see what boys were down there. You'd sit there and nurse a Sun Drop soda, craning your neck to see who walked in.

Thank goodness for the Haefner family. They accepted the fact that a lot of teenagers were going to be at the Wheel in the early evening hours. We understood that we should be out of there before the ballroom crowd showed up and actually spent money.

John and I started dating in high school and were married the day after I graduated college.

I wanted to marry a college graduate…I'm tempted to use all my old jokes here, but she'll say not to [laughter].

I married my best friend. He's my best friend. And that's it. And he's said that to me, and I've said that to him.

Kathy enriches my life in part because she is good at all sorts of things I'm not. I love all the quilts she's made, for instance. We have them all over the house. I'm just fascinated, because I can barely pound a nail into two boards and make them stay together. She can put all these little pieces of cloth together and a beautiful, colorful pattern emerges.

One of the things I tell people at wedding showers, you know, when you're supposed to write down some advice, is that there are peaks and valleys in any marriage. So when there are downs, don't just say "that's it"—recognize that's a valley, and that there is probably a peak after that valley.

Kathy and I spent most of our careers in education. Together we put in almost 60 years—Kathy as a teacher, and also with programs like Newspapers in Education and Mankato's Heart Health program. In addition to teaching, I served in the Minnesota Legislature from 1987-2006.

We both have similar philosophies of teaching, I think. Respecting each student. Respecting who they are and what they bring to the classroom, even those who might act up and might think they don't deserve any respect. When I taught, I really wanted to get to know students on a personal level—not everything about them, but enough that we could have a connection.

I think we agreed early on that we didn't teach the material but that we taught the student. The material helped all of us explore what we really thought, who we were, where we might be headed. At least that's what I thought I was doing. I have to laugh—one day I was out shopping and heard, "Mr. Dorn, how are you?" It was a former student. He introduced me to his wife, who asked, "What did you teach?" When I told her I was an English teacher, the guy didn't miss a beat. "Oh, is that what you were doing?" You can never be sure that the message you think you are sending is the one a student is receiving.

I think teachers get scapegoated. There are poor teachers, but the vast majority are very good. When you think about making it mandatory for everybody to attend school until they're a certain age, and how difficult it is to teach to all the different levels of ability and understanding, it's a monumental job. I just think teachers need more support, publicly, than they're getting.

I walked into the Wagon Wheel at some point in the 9th grade, and that connection then stayed in my life off and on ever since. When you're at the Wagon Wheel, you immediately get what people have on their minds. It's not filtered or structured. People are comfortable, so you hear what they have to say.

There are other gathering spots in the area. People gather at the Hy-Vee, for example, and that's important, too. But what the Wagon Wheel does is take you back a little bit in time and give you a feeling of the way maybe community was in a smaller town, in a different time. Support systems are there. Listening ears are there.

Mark Piepho

You have people in here from all walks of life, from the high to the low or whatever you want to call it. People come for the food, and the price is good, but they also come for the community of it. That's kind of what's neat to me—the community of it.

I'm in the moving and storage business. It's a family business that my dad started back in the early 1950s. I moved here in the winter of 1976 to help my brother get our Mankato location up and running. I did that full-time for a couple of years, and then I ran for the Legislature in 1978. '78 was a good year for Republicans, and I beat the incumbent. I was 26.

I served in the Minnesota House of Representatives for eight years. I won four elections and then lost to John Dorn in 1986 by 78 votes. In 1990 I won a special election for the Minnesota Senate and served until the end of the year. I ran again for State Senate in 2006, but did not pull it off. I served as Mayor of the city of Skyline for one term in the mid-1990s, and in 2008 I was elected to serve as a Blue Earth County Commissioner.

Overall in elections I think I'm seven and four. It's a lot easier and more fun to win—then you don't have to analyze why you didn't win. I keep running because of the idea of serving and helping people and just trying to make a difference in the world.

I used to get a little good-natured static here at the Wagon Wheel for being in the Legislature. They'd say things like, "What are you going to do to us today?" And somebody might razz me a little bit about the pay. But it was fun. I always liked coming here to chew the fat, and I still do.

I'm more worried about things now than I've ever been, and I'm a political junkie. In my view, the federal government has overreached. This isn't partisan, either. I think it's been going on for some time with Bush and Obama. All this "too big to fail," that's a bunch of crap, because failure is going to help most businesses out. When one fails or goes bankrupt, someone else buys them cheap. That's just how it works. I don't mean we shouldn't have any government, but you have to work to keep it limited. Government should always be the minority partner.

One thing I was especially proud of during my time in the Legislature was getting the new bridge in town named the Veterans Memorial Bridge. That was kind of neat because it was a bipartisan thing that gave some recognition to veterans of all wars fought. It's also kind of nice to see what is happening years after the bridge was named. They're working on a memorial real close to the bridge with markers and stuff. It's just cool.

The Wagon Wheel is just a great place to go and visit with people—people who are like you and people who are not.

Eric Anderson

When you come into the Wagon Wheel, there is no delineation as to who you are. Anyone who comes in this place and thinks they walk on a different level soon finds out they don't. This is the equalization place.

I was elected Mayor of Mankato in 2010. My wife still laughs about this. My friends do, too. "Why are you the Mayor?" I don't take myself too seriously. I'm the guy who many would have referred to as the class clown.

I do take my position as mayor seriously, though. I recognize there's a certain decorum that goes with my job. There are certain expectations of you as you represent the city. Being mayor does alter the way I carry myself in the community, but I believe it's important I never alter myself.

I like to hunt and fish, and I kind of take everything in stride and enjoy the day. I do have kind of a hankering for yesteryear, a soft spot in my heart for nostalgia. I like politics, but I'm bored by politicians. I guess I feel like I'm the typical local guy.

I'll be 45 in about a month. I'm a financial planner by trade. Like I tell my friends who are the same age as me, we're the adults now. It's taken me a long time to realize that. We're the ones that have to make sure the next generations have the same opportunities we've had.

My job as mayor isn't to sit down with the townsfolk and get into a battle over political issues. My job is to find out "what's your concern?" My job is to shut up, listen, observe, absorb and help Mankato remain a great town. It's the everyday conversations where I often learn the most, and for a long time the Haefners have operated a great place to hold them.

How would I define community? That's a tough question. I would say community is a place, a safe haven, where people can pursue their own lives with a sense of belonging. Community is a place where people feel comfortable and protected. The beauty of a community comes from all the different characters that are in it. To me, community is a house of characters.

There are a lot of places in town to go and have a good meal. But generally speaking, those are going to be more personal affairs. Your conversation is confined to your table. Here, I can turn around and yell at Kevin about the Twins or something, and no one is going to be offended that someone's shouting across the café.

The Wagon Wheel is the quintessential stomping ground for everyday life. It's not the event center. It's not the place that's going to host the big shindig. It's where everyday life takes place.

Marc Buchanan

Kevin, the owner of this place, makes it special. He just makes you feel at ease. Kevin is what they call a good Catholic boy. He does whatever he can to help people.

My mother was having a really hard time when I was born. She wasn't married and was just barely getting by. I ended up being raised by her parents, my grandparents. We lived in Iowa until I was about seven and then moved to Texas.

I didn't really do all that well in school. I got off to a slow start because of my coming from the North, and I was a slow learner too. When I was in reading class, I had a really tough teacher I still remember. She'd get mad at me and holler at me because I didn't read fast enough.

I went through the tenth grade in high school, and then I said, well, I'm going to join the military. I decided to join the Navy Reserve. Both my grandfather and my brother had served in the Army, so going into the military made sense to me.

This one high school teacher told me, he said, "You know what, you might think you're going to go into the Navy and it's going to be a picnic, but you got another thing coming. It ain't going to be no picnic." Boy, I found that to be true about the first couple of days [laughing].

I was in the Navy for two years. I was at sea on the aircraft carrier *Midway* for 18 months. We went to Hawaii, Japan, the Philippines, and Hong Kong. I really enjoyed the Navy, but I just didn't have the discipline to stay, you know. I kept thinking, boy, I could get back out on the outside in the civilian world and just have so much more freedom and everything. I left the Navy in February of 1965.

Things didn't go so well after the military. After I got out I just didn't have no discipline. From 1965 to 1982, I worked off and on as a longshoremen in Houston, Texas. I also worked on some construction jobs and even tried being a roofer for a while. I was drinking a lot during those years and dealing with anxiety and depression too.

I've been sober 25 years now. It's wonderful. Your whole life changes. My sister once told me, "You know, you may not have been real successful in your work history and everything, but quitting drinking is a good thing that you did." And it is. I'm real proud of getting sober. People have a lot more respect for you, and they don't make fun of you. People used to make fun of me for how drunk I got.

I know a lot of alcoholics on the street. I help them out however I can. They see me and know I don't drink. I've had a couple of them tell me that they appreciate that and give me credit for not drinking. I hope some of them see me and know it's possible for them to get sober, too.

I'm a Kennedy man, you know. When I was in the military, John F. Kennedy was my Commander in Chief until November 22, 1963, when he was assassinated. His dad instilled in him that to whom much is given, much is expected. I think the people that have the real good capabilities and the real high intelligence who are able to get up in status in everything—I think they should help people that are less fortunate. If I was rich, I'd be like Warren Buffett. I think he has a genuine desire to help the country in any way he can.

The Wagon Wheel helps me with my depression and anxiety. I know I can always come in here and talk with Kevin about the Twins or talk with the other people I know down here. It kind of gives you self-esteem and confidence, too—to be able to talk to the people here.

"Much humor within third places plays on a characteristic of *im*politeness, which really communicates affection. It does so with humor and has the advantage of credibility in a world where so much politeness is pro forma."

Ray Oldenburg—*The Great Good Place*

Michelle Fasnacht

My mom worked at the Wagon Wheel when I was a kid back in the 1960s and 1970s. Kevin's dad Wally hired her and said she was one of the best waitresses he had. After school I'd come down here and wait for my mom to get done working so we could go home together. Wally would give me cookies and milk while I waited in one of the booths.

I'm a housekeeper at Good Counsel here in Mankato. I've been there 28 years. I work with the sisters, and I really like it. It's not tense like other jobs. Whenever you have a birthday or you're ill or something, they'll say happy birthday, they'll pray for you. The sisters make it like you're family up there. They make it fun.

I like to clean. You accomplish something every day, and the sisters praise it because they like it clean, and it smells clean. You keep the sisters from getting sick when you keep it clean.

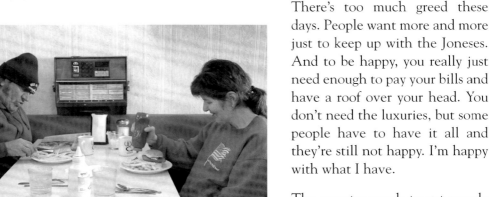

I had math and reading problems in school. I went to several schools and just couldn't adjust. I ended up going to school at Good Counsel. It was a place for girls who needed help with learning or if they were having other troubles. I liked it there because the atmosphere was better and I could get along. I could study better. They would help you out there more than the other schools would. I learned how to read better, how to cope with life and everything else. I graduated in 1979.

I get along with people, and I like to help people. I help the homeless as much as I can, and I used to work at the food shelf. It makes me feel good when I do things for other people, and I know God's happy that I helped out.

There's too much greed these days. People want more and more just to keep up with the Joneses. And to be happy, you really just need enough to pay your bills and have a roof over your head. You don't need the luxuries, but some people have to have it all and they're still not happy. I'm happy with what I have.

The country needs to get people back to work. There are too many people out of jobs. And when they're out of jobs, then we have people bickering so much about it. They need to start hiring people so that people can be happier.

When I was a kid, it felt good to come to the Wagon Wheel because it was like a family place. That's why I came back so many times and why I still come back. You feel like it's home.

Dan Johnson

The waitresses at the Wagon Wheel are good about helping us guys in chairs, whatever we need. I feel real good when I come into the Wagon Wheel. It feels like home.

I like to get out and meet people in the community. You will have to correct me if I'm wrong, but interacting with people is really important, I think. I don't want to just stay in my apartment getting old. At the Wagon Wheel I'm always talking with Kevin and Johnny Harrington about sports. I've always been sports to the max.

I was the wrestling manager in high school. I wanted to get involved with sports, and I knew the coach pretty well. So one day after school I went to his practice and he suggested I become the team manager. I had to be at every practice. I carried a whistle, too, so I had a big job [laughs].

I knew right away, probably when I was a baby, that I wasn't going to be able to walk. I've had cerebral palsy since I was born. There are several kinds of it. Mine, I was very lucky, it did not affect my mind, only my legs pretty much.

I don't want anybody to feel sorry for me. I don't want anybody thinking, "Oh, Dan is in a chair, that's too bad for him." It was a fluke and it happens, so I have to deal with it. And I deal with it pretty well. I do have my moments when I get depressed, just like anybody else. We are all human. But being in a chair is OK. I adapted really well.

One of my aides coaches basketball and brings me to his practices and games. The kids on the team know me well now, and they sit down and talk with me sometimes. I like that. I value talking to the kids so they don't get so afraid, because a lot of kids get afraid of people in chairs, you know. I haven't really asked them, but they seem to like me.

I used to go up to the college with a friend of mine and talk with students who really wanted to learn about disabilities. We would talk to classes for hours. They would ask what it was like to be in a chair, how did we react to things and stuff like that. I enjoyed talking with the college students. It was nice knowing people cared about me and my experiences.

Baseball season just started, so that is all we talk about now at the Wagon Wheel. Baseball, baseball, baseball…

Dear Richard,
We have an excess of tator tot hotdish, tator tots, and chicken noodle soup! Hope all is well and miss ya!

Alissa Haney-White

When I walk in the door of the Wagon Wheel, I honestly feel everyone's energy. I hit the door and woosh—it's a whirlwind of emotions. Maybe somebody's having a good day or somebody's having a bad day. I feel all that. I like that sense of feeling. It's a real blessing to have all these people in here.

I'm on my third go-around as a waitress at the Wagon Wheel. I left a couple times for management jobs at other restaurants, but as soon as I hit that position I felt like I lost something. You don't have contact with the customers anymore. It took me all these years to figure out I don't need to move up.

I'm like that kid that leaves home a couple of times but ends up coming back. I think I'm here for good this time. The first and second time I worked here I didn't always have the best attitude. I was like, I'm just here to take your order. This third time around has just been amazing. Now it's more like "how are the grandkids" or "how's business," you know. I talk with the customers about just about everything.

I was a bad, bad high school student [laughs]. I was a wild child. My junior and senior year I never cracked a book. I went all the way to my last day, but I still didn't graduate.

My performance in school all changed after my mom died. She's been gone . . . it'll be 20 years this December. We lost her when I was 13. She was 37. I pretty much was born knowing she had cancer, so I grew up with that. As soon as she was gone, it was like my world was gone. I was at the point where I was just starting to grow up, and she was missing that. It was like, well, this really sucks because she's not here. She doesn't get to see me do this or that. So I didn't care. I just stopped caring one day.

My mom was an amazing person. Always vivacious, always active. Even at her sickest time she was still moving and still going no matter what. She wanted to keep on trucking.

At one point I was nothing like my mom in how I approached life. But now I can actually relate to her. Now I keep on going and I keep active. She enjoyed life to the fullest, and as I've gotten older, that's what I'm looking for. I want to do everything.

Three years after high school, I got my diploma, my GED. I've taken courses in massage therapy, and I'm thinking of someday doing that part-time or on the side. I almost always have two waitressing or bartending jobs going at the same time. I work about 60 hours a week. I'm 33 now, and I feel like I'm really starting to evolve.

The Wagon Wheel is like my world. I look forward to these people every day. If I didn't have them, I don't know what I'd do. I really don't. They give me crap, I give them crap. It's beautiful. It's not a stretch at all to say this place is helping me become a better person.

Rebel Miller

I have worn a step meter in here, and in an eight-hour shift I average ten miles, so I get my exercise, but I don't consider it hard work. I've been at the Wagon Wheel ten years, and I love working here.

I enjoy helping people—at the Wagon Wheel and everywhere else. I'm the one who puts the Band-Aid on everybody, kisses all the boo-boos, and tries to make everybody feel better. I started out working in nursing homes, and for six years I was an Emergency Medical Technician on an ambulance. Taking care of people is almost ingrained in me.

I was born in Minnesota but raised in Oklahoma, and I've been back and forth my whole life. I was a teenager when I had my three children and got married for the first time. I was divorced before I was 20, and then kind of raised my kids on my own. I'm 38 now, and the kids are 23, 22, and the youngest will be 21 in September.

All three of my kids have graduated and made it to adulthood without becoming parents, which is something I worked to teach them was important. I think they saw my struggle, too, and realized it wasn't a road they wanted to try. I'm very proud of them.

My mom is the closest person in the world to me. She taught me that if I don't have something nice to say, I shouldn't say anything at all. One time a man here complained about the size of the soda we include in the price of our meals: "It isn't even a swallow" was what he said. I told him, "Well, that's why you can afford the meal for $3.64." I felt so bad that I called my mom and told her I snapped at this customer today, and she said, "You're old enough, Rebel, if you feel you need to say something you can say it."

I've been on a pursuit of sorts lately. I signed up for a Psychic Potpourri class where we study things like Astrology, Numerology, and Tarot. I also just recently got out my mother's *Holy Bible* that she has passed on to me, and I intend to read it. As I get older, I am seeking to enlighten myself more about things beyond what we see in this world and trying to interpret my own viewpoint on things.

What do I like most about the job? Visiting with the customers. I've got children that I've watched grow up for the past ten years. With some of my older regulars, just a pat on the back or a touch on the shoulder seems to bring them peace. That is wonderfully fulfilling. I think the fact that we've been here 60 years matters to people. They always know we will be here.

"Yet even those profits of participation
that seem most personal
are never wholly so,
for whatever improves social creatures
improves their relations with others.
What the third place contributes
to the whole person
may be counted as a boon to all."

Ray Oldenburg—*The Great Good Place*

Denise Premeau

Back in 1992, I answered Kevin's ad, and it went like this: "Needed, soup-maker and pie-baker at the Wagon Wheel." I went in and applied, and I got the job. I showed him I knew what I was doing.

I grew up in a larger family. We were very poor. When I was eight years old, my mom had twin boys and all the other kids were assigned a specific job. Mine was cooking. So at eight years old, I'd push my chair up to the stove and make a meal for everybody. I made the same kinds of things we serve at the Wagon Wheel—goulash, meat loaf, chow mein and spaghetti to name a few.

I don't measure nothing. It's a dash of this and a scoop of that. People have asked me for recipes and stuff and I say, "Well, I can't really give it to you…you're just going to have to watch me make it and figure out what it is" [laughs].

I enjoy cooking because you can see the results in a short amount of time, and then you feel an accomplishment. It's a small thing, but it's a positive thing. All my life I've tried to hang on to the positive things.

The highlight of my life right now is that I'm a grandma. I dearly love my little granddaughter—she's eight years old now, going on 18 mentally. We have a special bond because I was my daughter's birth coach. I got to be the one the doctor handed the baby to. It was like the ultimate high to watch my granddaughter be born and to be there for my daughter.

I've been on my own since I was 16. I hit the road because I realized that my home life was different than everybody else's. I lived in group homes, I lived in foster homes, I lived with friends and family. I learned you can do anything if you put your mind do it—*anything*. I put myself through high school and through a lot of different things up until today.

I started selling Avon when my daughter was six months old—28 years ago. We had nothing—nothing. I went to my purse and dug out as much change as I could. Then I robbed her piggy bank and came up with the twenty bucks I needed to start. My first order was only $35, but the next order was something like $235 and I paid some bills with it. Today I'm the top selling Avon lady in Mankato—I have been for a few years. I have somewhere between three and four hundred customers.

Avon has a lot to do with my becoming a stronger person. I have goals with Avon, and I think that's what everyone needs—they need a goal. When they think that they're just spinning their tires and not going anywhere in life, it's because they don't have a goal. When you don't have a goal, what are you doing? You're just wasting time.

What do I feel like when I walk in the Wagon Wheel? That I'm needed. That I have a purpose to start my day, a reason to get out of bed. Somebody is always asking me to bake them their birthday cookies or calling to see what the soup of the day is. They always want to know what I'm making.

You walk into the Wagon Wheel and there's a lawyer sitting next to a farmer sitting next to high school students sitting next to a nurse. There's always a mixture of people, and that's what makes the place so special. It's like my recipes—a little bit of this and a little bit of that. Put it all together and it comes out right.

Lisa Beck

Coming in the Wagon Wheel feels like coming home. You just feel comfortable. You walk in and everybody says hi. You start picking on people, or you get picked on, the minute you walk in the door. I'm usually taking orders before I even get my apron on.

Every day here is just a little bit different. It's the same people every day, but there's always something new. Same soap opera, new episode [laughs].

I moved to Mankato in 1984 to attend Mankato State University. I went to MSU for three years. Originally, I was majoring in international relations, then I switched over to international business, then I decided I just didn't want to go to college anymore. I felt like I was just spinning my wheels. Honestly, I went because my dad wanted me to. It wasn't where I wanted to be.

I had a variety of jobs around town after I left MSU. I worked at a parking ramp, then I worked at a couple of different gas stations and a couple of bars, then I worked here at the Wagon Wheel for my first time. I started here in 1992 and left in 1995.

On my 30th birthday, I decided I should go back to college because I was like, "OK, I should get a degree and a job with benefits." So I went to Rasmussen College and got a degree in Business Management and Travel and Tourism.

I wanted to be a travel agent, but about the time I graduated, Internet travel was taking off and they weren't hiring travel agents anymore. I did work for three years in the travel industry, at a call center where you've got a headset on and it's just a voice at the other end. I didn't like that. I like a face-to-face human contact job where you can actually see the person you're giving customer service to.

I started working at the Wagon Wheel again in July of 2010. You get to know people when you work here. You talk to them about their lives, their day-to-day worries, their grocery lists [laughs]. When a regular customer has something good happen, you celebrate with them. When a regular customer or a member of their family passes away, you go through the grief process with them because you've lost a member of the Wagon Wheel family.

I love to travel. It's my favorite pastime when I have time off and can afford it. I've been to Ireland twice. The second time I went, I took myself over there on my 40th birthday. It was like, I'm going back to Ireland—that's what I'm going to do for my 40th birthday. So I saved up for five years to go back. I didn't know anybody on the tour, but I made new friends from Australia, England, and the U.S. It's beautiful over there. There really are 40 different shades of green.

My dad wasn't happy with my decision to leave college, but when I talk to him now he'll say that I'm the most grounded of all his children, and that he's proud of me because I stood up for what I believed in and I found what makes me happy.

If it's a really stressful day down here, one of the regulars will come in and crack a joke and it just kind of lightens the mood. You step back and laugh and say, "OK, now on with the show."

Dave Bottin

You sit down in the Wagon Wheel and you could be right beside a judge, a police officer, or a bus driver. You respect everybody and they respect you. It's not, "I'm sorry, Your Honor," no, at the Wagon Wheel it's first names.

My grandfather served during World War II, but he never really spoke about it. Then, not long after he passed away in 1980, we found this *Reader's Digest,* and in there was a picture of General MacArthur pinning the Bronze Star on my grandfather. That kind of put a pride into me that you don't have to be loud and boisterous, that you can do very good things in a very quiet way.

I enlisted in the Marines in 1983, before I even graduated high school. I was in for five years, one month, and 14 days—not that I counted. Blew my knee out, and that ended my active duty. When I came back to civilian life, the backstabbing and selfishness was just overwhelming to me. You have such camaraderie and you build such a trust in the military. It's rough being out. I still have problems now. As the saying goes: Once a Marine, always a Marine.

After the Marines, I spent about seven years in the National Guard and did odd jobs outside the military. I built windows, drove truck, worked in die-casting. Then I went to college. I received my Associate's Degree, and I was going to MSU to get my Bachelor's Degree until I had a heart attack.

At first it felt like I had a big belch that I couldn't get rid of. I had just gotten out of class when I started getting the pains shooting down my arms. It was painful to even touch my arms against my body. Then the tightness started in my shoulders, and that's when I knew for sure it was a heart attack. I think I was 38.

After they got me stabilized in the hospital, I called my ex-wife, and I told her I wanted to see my son, who was about three then. The horror look on his face, to see his dad in a hospital bed with things connected to him, just devastated me. I was a smoker back then. My favorite thing my son said is, "Daddy, you got to stop those ickies because I don't want you to have another heart attack." I smoked up until February of 2005. I got so upset I threw my cigarettes against the wall, and I have not touched one since. It's how bad do you really want things.

I come down to the Wagon Wheel and Rebel and the other waitresses know some of my past. They'll sit there and say, "Now, can you have that pie today?" or "How's your sugar count?" Damn, I've got more wives than a person is allowed, and I'm not even married. But they care for you and want to see you come back.

Brad Walker

The Wagon Wheel is a place where you literally can leave your job or your title at the door. That's important to me because of my personality. I happen to be a judge, but I don't want that to define me as a person.

When I get here, most of the time it's 5:30 in the morning and I'm one of the first customers. There are a couple other regulars here that early in the morning, and we joke around, talk about the crossword puzzle, or somebody might mention how I made the paper again. It feels like a comfortable old shoe.

I was in the Marines a total of almost 34 years. I signed up in 1967 when I was a freshman in college. Immediately following law school, I spent four years active duty as a lawyer, and when I got out I stayed active in the reserves. I got called up for Desert Storm and ended up spending six months on active duty as a Support Squadron Commanding Officer. I retired as a Colonel when I took the bench as a judge about 14 years ago.

I think the Marine Corps, or any branch of the service, doesn't really teach you to be a certain way, but it shows you that if you work hard, if you pay attention to detail, and if you treat others with respect, that you're going to get that treatment back. I tried to treat my troops with respect, and I do the same when somebody comes before me as a judge.

I see being a judge as, for the most part, a form of public service. Most people make far more money practicing law than being a judge. I guess it sounds hackneyed to say, but I see my job as an opportunity to give back to the community.

My toughest decisions are in child-related cases. Taking away a child from a parent, who may love that child very much, but who is incapable of parenting because of mental illness, chemical dependency, or other issues is a very tough decision. It's a daunting task when you have to write down on an order that a person's rights to their child are terminated.

I've been on a bowling league for a number of years. Some of us on the team have been together for 20 or 25 years, I think. I work hard at it, and I've had pretty good success. My average this year is about 220. I had one 300 game in my life a number of years ago. That was kind of a highlight, but you keep striving for that perfect game every single time.

The reason I've worked hard for whatever success I've had in life is because I didn't want to disappoint my parents. I wanted to do well so that they were proud of me, and I believe I accomplished that. I've managed to get to this age, and I don't think I've done anything that has embarrassed them, which is really what you try to do in life. The last thing you want to do is have them need to answer for something you did.

The Wagon Wheel is one of the places where you maintain being grounded in the community. You see people here from all walks of life—sometimes at their best and sometimes not at their best. But even if you're having a bad day, you can have a friendly cup of coffee with the folks here and try to figure out that it's going to be a little bit better tomorrow.

"It is a fortunate aspect
of the third place that its capacity to serve
the human need
for communion does not much depend
upon the capacity of a nation
to comprehend its virtues."

Ray Oldenburg—*The Great Good Place*

LOWELL & JEAN JOHNSON

Editor's Note – Jean Johnson's comments are in italics.

I'm Lowell Johnson. I've been coming here since 1951. It was kind of a high school hangout in those days.

I've been coming here for, oh, the last 40 years I guess. . . . What makes the place special? I think it's the eclectic mix of people that come in. You have the suits, followed by the tattoos and the piercings, and just the everyday person. It's just fun to see such a mix of people.

And the price is right.

Lowell and I got married in 1969. We have two daughters: Jackie by Lowell's first marriage and Kim from my first marriage. The kids are 48 and 49 now. They were seven and eight when we got married. We told them in the car outside Lowell's parents' house that we were going to get married, and they said, "Oooh, we'll be sisters."

We're used to each other's faults. We take turns letting the other person have their way. She lets me do most the talking, though [laughs].

I like the way he thinks and the way he does things. We enjoy many of the same activities, and we just enjoy each other's company.

We still camp out. We have a pop-up camper, and we camped out for over a month this summer. Since we've retired, we've taken three Amtrak trips and covered pretty much the entire U.S. The train lets us relax and see everything. We also get the chance to meet and talk with new people.

Right now our life is changing. We just got a new little kitty. It's just a little stray that walked up to an aunt's farm, about ten weeks old. If either one of us thought we were the boss of the house, we've learned now that the kitty is [laughs].

I think everybody can benefit from getting involved in the community. Jean and I call Bingo one Sunday a month at seniors' home over in North Mankato, and we put together our church newsletter every other Wednesday. Jean is on the Memorials Committee at church and volunteers at the Summit Center for seniors. I was a volunteer firefighter for years. I still serve in the beer garden at events [laughs]. For us, being involved in the community is kind of selfish too, because you do it in part because you enjoy it so much.

I just enjoy getting myself involved with things. You meet new people, enjoy them, and do some good. I guess maybe a person should pick out a couple things to do in the community that they really enjoy. If it isn't working out, drop it and go on to the next thing that's more enjoyable.

I'm 76, and I'm really lucky to get to this age with all the things that have gone on. They've saved my life several times over there at the Mayo Clinic. They do a super job. I've had prostate cancer and an abdominal aortic aneurism. I've also had about seven bouts with thyroid cancer over the years. I have only one vocal cord, which sometimes makes it difficult to talk, but I guess you have to play the cards you're dealt.

It hasn't slowed him down at all…I still have trouble keeping him quiet! Seriously though, these kinds of things help you learn to pick and choose what is important in your life—the things you can disregard and the things you have to take seriously.

They get to know you at the Wagon Wheel. When I come in, I just say, "I'll have my breakfast," and they know what it is: Two eggs basted, sausage, and whole wheat toast.

The Wagon Wheel is the hometown place to go. You know so many people that come in and you visit with them. You always feel kind of "up" after you leave here.

Sandie Blekestad

I worked at the Wagon Wheel in the late 1960s. I really enjoyed working here, and I've been coming back ever since. When you walk into the Wagon Wheel, you feel the old times, the good times when things weren't so stressful, you know. Yeah, it gets loud and it gets noisy, but that's all part of it.

My kids and my grandkids are my whole world. I've got four kids and 13 grandchildren. I was married twice, divorced twice, and I more or less raised the kids by myself because my partners in life were not a good choice.

I did a lot of waitressing work out of high school. Then I worked for Onan Electronics for about 13 years. I worked at Johnson Outdoors for another ten years, until I retired because of physical problems.

After I retired, it got to the point where I could not afford my apartment anymore, so I ended up moving in with my daughter and her three children. She is a single mother who works in housekeeping, and you just can't afford daycare, rent, and everything else on that salary. My daughter and I get along very well, and I'm glad to help out with the kids. I mean, there are times when she tells me, "Mom, just be quiet, they're my kids and I'm home now. I can take care of it." Grandma does have her opinion—she does—but overall there's no strain there or anything.

The kids are so fun. I call my little five-year-old "monkey boy" because he climbs everything. I caught him climbing the shed the other day [laughs]. Last night there was a friend over, and all they did was run back and forth through the trailer—just as fast as they could go, chasing each other around. They just make every day something new.

I think our economy is going to the dogs. I do. People cannot make it anymore. They sit there and say, "It's going to turn, the economy is turning around." Well, I just don't see it. What can be done about it? Oh, man. Start giving people the wages they deserve for one thing. The minimum wage has to go up. I mean, it takes two or three people now to work in order to make it, and that's why you have so many families moving in together now.

People in government need to walk in our shoes for about a week and see how it feels, because right now they have no clue what we go through. But they won't degrade themselves. They've got so much money and so much influence, that they don't think they need to come down here and see exactly what's going on in the real world.

I'm really proud of the fact that my kids have grown up to be the kind of people they have. They're hard-working and they take good care of their kids. They've had their problems in life; but who hasn't, you know? And they've come through them. My kids are just fantastic—and so are my grandkids.

You know, that guy sitting over there at the end of the counter is one of the regulars who used be in here when I worked here in the 60s. He's sitting in the same spot he always sat in, too.

Tammy Phillips

Growing up, I spent a lot of time on Front Street, and to see some of the people I knew then still here at the Wagon Wheel means a lot. Things seemed so simple back then. Maybe that's what you hang on to when you walk into the Wagon Wheel.

My first job was at Pizza Kato, just a couple doors down from the Wagon Wheel. I was 15 when I started back in 1975. I saw the bar rush, the Harley riders, and the high schoolers who poured salt into pepper and pepper into salt. I saw the families on Sundays, and I saw the way some of the homeless and struggling people on Front Street were treated with respect and not condemned. I learned social skills on Front Street, and my upbringing down here molded me into who I am today.

I took typing in high school, and I got a "D." I knew if I'm a woman I have to know how to type, so I took the class again. This time I got an "F." How can you fail typing? Me, I cheated—I looked at the keyboard because the coordination wasn't working for me. I realized even back then that, as life changed and we got more into technology, it wasn't going to be my thing.

Fast-forward 35 years, and I own Midwest Insurance Group here in Mankato. We work with senior citizens to help them navigate through this maze we call Medicare. I love that my older clients know more than I do about life, and I love that I get to learn from what they've done. Often, we talk for 15-20 minutes about insurance, and the rest of the time we're having conversations about them or their families or whatever they want to talk about. Sometimes I'm the first person they've talked to face-to-face in three weeks. I'm not in any hurry. It's ok. Young people want it emailed. They can buy it on the Internet. I enjoy sitting on my butt and talking to my customers.

I cannot express the feeling that I get, having a license allowing me to sign a piece of paper that can change somebody's life. Maybe it's a life insurance policy on their loved one when they pass away. There are a lot of things that come with grief in that situation that I can't do anything about. But I can be there with a wheelbarrowful of money that can take some of the weight off their shoulders. And I think, I did that. I helped with that by helping them make a decision 5, 10, or 20 years ago. It's boring. It's guaranteed. But they'll have it.

My 26-year-old daughter just started in the insurance business with me. She majored in Spanish and International Business up at MSU, and went to work for a marketing firm. She was doing very well, but one day she came to me and said, "Mom, I think I want to learn your business. You enjoy what you're doing and you have fun—I want to have fun." The other day she saw me typing an email and informed me we should film me typing and send it to funniest home videos. "We'd win for sure," she said. And we might—my typing is still a hoot.

There's noise at the Wagon Wheel. Everybody's here. We're losing places like this, and I think what we're losing is that feeling of community that you get walking in here. It's not stressful. It's not "please wait to be seated." It's just a feeling of simplicity and comfort.

Kenny DeWitte

The place feels like home, it really does. I get the same thing most every time I'm here. For breakfast, it's always an omelet with whole wheat toast and American fries. For lunch, it's a bowl of soup, a ham salad sandwich and a Coca-Cola.

The accident happened on Saturday, September 25th, 2004, at 5:15 in the afternoon. I think that's when church starts, 5:15. The driver of the car turned left off the country road into the church parking lot—no turn signals, just abruptly turned. My 13-year-old daughter and I were on my Harley coming down the road, probably doing sixty miles an hour. All I could tell her is, "Hang on, we're going to crash."

My daughter went 95 feet, cartwheeling down the road. She had four broken thoracic vertebrae, a broken ankle, and a lot of road rash. The helmet saved her life. I went straight over the roof of the car. Busted me up pretty good. They had me in an induced coma for 35 days. I was in the hospital for over 100 days, and put in another four months of physical therapy.

I believe in the power of prayer from this thing, I'll tell you that. I started seeing these printouts and emails from people saying, "Kenny was put on our list today; we are praying for him." It was just astronomical. They had a fundraiser over at the church and over 900 people showed up. It was an unbelievable feeling to think that 900 people showed up for me and my family.

My daughter is doing well today. She just finished cosmetology school up at the Aveda Institute. This is a daughter haircut right here—she's cut it twice now.

I still have chronic pain from the accident. My injuries were bad enough that I could have gone on disability from Social Security, but I didn't do it. What's a person going to do with themselves? Me, I went back to work as soon as I could. And I got a new Harley.

I've been a working-class guy my whole life. Working-class means you get a little dirt under your fingernails. I work at Crown Beverage Packaging and have for 26 years. We make can tops. Work gives me an opportunity to prove to everybody that I'm capable of doing what I'm doing. It's not about the can tops, it's about going there and dealing with what is put in front of you every day.

I served on the North Mankato City Council for four years, from 2007 to 2010. Why did I do it? I was a Boy Scout and an Eagle Scout. You get the Citizenship Merit Badge, you know. But then years later you find yourself sitting with somebody complaining about things over coffee or a beer—"they" are doing this and "they" are doing that. Well, you can go one step further, get your hat in the ring and get involved.

I was ecstatic when I got elected. I was just in Heaven. In high school I wasn't one of the people on the honor role or anything like that. I ran for class office a couple of times, but I was never the winner. I was the guy in last place. Here was an opportunity to serve my community, to represent my neighbors and others throughout town.

I haven't accomplished everything I wanted to in life, but I thank the Lord I am here to enjoy what is left of it. I hope I can endure into my senior years. Heck, I guess I'm classified as a senior now—I'm soon to be 56.

"Precious and unique benefits accrue
to those who regularly attend third places
and who value those forms of
social intercourse found there.
The leveling, primacy of conversation,
certainty of meeting friends,
looseness of structure,
and eternal reign of the imp of fun
all combine to set the stage for experiences
unlikely to be found elsewhere."

Ray Oldenburg—*The Great Good Place*

Dennis Bents

I live close to the Wagon Wheel—about seven or eight blocks away. I come here about five mornings a week during the school year. It's cheap and it's close to the bus stop.

I grew up on a farm. It was hard work, but I enjoyed the cattle, the pigs, and doing the chores. I remember being around seven or eight, getting off the bus and going into the house to put on my everyday clothes to do the cattle and the pigs. I liked it.

School was all right. Math, I was pretty good at it. English I was somewhat good at it. Social Studies I was all right, I guess. I got all D's or F's in shop—I wasn't good at it.

I didn't get done with school on time. I went to a special class. I don't know what they call it—where you finish up if you get behind or something.

I just turned 53 on March 15. I've been in town since 1978, I suppose. When I first moved here I lived in a boarding home, but I didn't really feel like I belonged in one. I guess some other people thought that too. I've lived on my own for over 25 years now.

I work up at the college. I'm a dishwasher in one of the dorms. I think it's going on seven years I've been there. The job keeps me hoppin' [laughs]. I used to work at a hotel making beds and cleaning rooms. I liked it, but those beds were so low and you had to make them just so right, just perfect. It was hard on my back. I couldn't do it no more.

I am a quiet person. I don't know why, I just am. I used to talk a lot, but then I stopped talking because it seemed like people thought I was saying the wrong thing or something. I don't know, that's how I felt. Like they didn't want to listen. I like to come in the Wagon Wheel and just listen to all the junk that goes on. I kind of feel part of the conversation here. I get kind of a smile from listening.

Country music is my favorite. I was born in the country, so I just stuck to that music, I guess. I think I have about 72 CDs—I got the whole rack filled up. When I listen to a country song it kind of unwinds me, you know. Laurie Anderson, Brad Paisley, the Statler Brothers, Tayna Tucker—there's a lot of them I like.

I'm proud that I went on from school and showed other people that I can do what I do. I can be on my own, do the bills, keep a job, stuff like that. I try to go faster on the stuff I was slower at. That's the main thing, I guess. I'm trying to talk more, too.

I just kind of like this place. I don't know exactly the words.

Don Aaker

I come to the Wagon Wheel just about every day for lunch. I look forward to coming down. You forget about what's going on outside, and you're just kind of watching what's going on inside. It's really relaxing and enjoyable.

I can't ever remember not wanting to go into the Marine Corps. I joined as soon as I turned 17. I did what I was told. I went where I was told. You sign your name on the paper, that's a binding contract that says you will do what your country wants you to do. No questions.

My biological father was divorced from my mother when I was very young. He was a Corporal in the Army during World War II. He was something else. He ended up being killed in Italy. I was nine when he died. I remember my mother called me in the house and told me. It kind of broke me up for a while.

Four or five years ago, I had a friend who went over to Italy for vacation. My dad is buried about 20 miles outside of Rome, so I asked my friend if he would be willing to go down there and get me some pictures. He did. That was the first time I had seen the grave marker with my dad's name on there and that. He's in a beautiful cemetery.

I had two fathers growing up, so I was lucky. My stepfather raised me since I was three years old. I always considered him my dad, and I introduced him as my dad. He worked hard his entire life. He didn't ask anybody for anything. He worked for it. He drove truck around Duluth and Superior—never complained, never griped.

I did three stints in the Marines. I was in from 1951–1954, then out for three months. I went back in from 1954–1959 and left so I could spend more time with my family. That wasn't working out so good, so I figured I'd go back into the Marine Corps. I went in again in 1967, and stayed until 1986. I was in long enough that I served in both the Korean War and the Vietnam War.

After the Marines, I worked at Minnesota State University from 1986 until 1998, mostly in campus security. I liked the job, but the kind of camaradarie you have in the Marines doesn't exist in civilian life. It just ain't out here.

What am I proudest of? Making Sargent Major in the Marine Corps. I couldn't go any higher. It's as high as you can go as an enlisted Marine. I think that's my proudest accomplishment. I love the Marines every bit as much right now as I did in the 1950s and 60s or whenever. It's part of my life. It is my life. I would go back tomorrow if they'd take me.

I ended up with prostate cancer a few years ago and had it taken care of. It was a shocker but, you know, so many of us came down with so many different things from that Agent Orange they used over there that I guess I could've figured it. I'm not saying that's what caused my cancer, but I wonder. They didn't know what it would do to you in those days. I guess somebody should have checked it out a little more before they used it, but it's part of war. It's part of the life I accepted.

I'm 77, but I still feel 30. I'm going to enjoy things while I'm here. Life is short. Sometimes I go outside and I just overdo it, you know, because I still feel so good—but the body is not quite 30 anymore.

I think every town should have a kind of watering hole or meeting place, and there's a great one at the Wagon Wheel. You meet a lot of nice people here.

Jim Pfau

The Wagon Wheel is a hometown restaurant with good food, but what I really like about it is the people. The different stories you hear and the things that people say. There's a close-knittedness you feel when you come in here.

I'm part of the 8:00 a.m. coffee group that meets before the Bullshippers. My dad, Jim Pfau Sr., used to be part of the same group, and I started coming in with him when I was in high school. It was really interesting listening to the old-timers' stories and seeing the camamradarie between everybody in the group.

My dad passed away in 1984. There was a short period where I stopped coming down, but then I decided to start coming back again. No specific reason per se. It just felt good seeing the guys and talking about different things—fishing, golf, whatever. Sometimes they would tell stories about my dad, and it was nice to hear those, you know.

The majority of the buildings on Front Street where the Wagon Wheel sits were taken down during urban renewal. I think a lot of people at the Wagon Wheel come together and share memories of what was once here on Front Street. I know our group has certainly talked about that on many occasions—*what was that old building that used to be down on such and such…* I think sharing these memories is important for people. It keeps people going, you know.

I'm sure my dad wanted to pass down to me the tradition of coming to the Wagon Wheel to eat, socialize, and learn how to get along with people. That's what I'm doing, and I enjoy it or I wouldn't be doing it. I think you have to learn how to communicate with people verbally and personally. I think that could be a potential problem with our youth. They do a lot of texting, and I guess that's a form of communication, but it's missing a lot. Down here, it's still the old-school way of communicating.

Tell you about myself? There's not too much to tell. I was born and raised in Mankato. I got into the real estate business in 1987 and have been doing that ever since. I have a passion for music. I've been playing the violin with the Mankato Symphony Orchestra for 32 years now. I am an Eagle Scout, and am very involved with the Boy Scouts—actually, I'm president of that board right now. I served two terms as president of the Realtors Association of Southern Minnesota. I'm a past president of the orchestra board.

I think you have to give back to the community what it gives to you. Not everyone has to contribute to the community in the same way. Some can give money, some can give time, but I think those who don't give back are missing out on an important part of life. If they did give back, I think they'd realize how much fun it is to contribute to your community. Being involved with any aspect of the community helps you see the positives you have in life.

Our coffee group talks about the same old boring thing every day, but yet there's always something new. The whole group is a positive group. We talk about serious things sometimes, but we laugh a lot. You need to have laughter, and that's what this group does. We laugh a lot.

Jerry Schuck

I started coming to the Wagon Wheel in high school, over 50 years ago. It was a very popular high school hangout. This was back in the 1950s—we're talking leather jackets, poodle dresses, and ducktail hairdos. The Everly Brothers and Jerry Lee Lewis on the jukebox.

You'd come into the Wagon Wheel after cruising Front Street, and you'd visit with whoever was here. It was quite a gathering spot. I believe I came here every single day of the year. I remember I was a little disgusted they were closed on Christmas and Easter.

I graduated high school in 1958. Ten days after graduation, I enlisted in the Navy. I was 17. I went to San Francisco, got assigned to an aircraft carrier, and went overseas. We had no war going on, so I was cruising around in the South Pacific. I made Hawaii, Guam, Japan, Okinawa, Hong Kong…I saw the world.

After the Navy, I decided I liked California. I'd seen the Rose Parade and knew it was 10 or 20 below here in Minnesota, so that made some decisions for me. I married soon after returning to the states and spent the next 45 years in California. My wife and I had three children, and I worked in printing and real estate.

My wife and I divorced after 45 years of marriage, and in 2003 I moved home to spend more time with my aging parents. I felt like I missed out on something in my relationship with my parents, because I was gone so long. I came home to make up—well, not make up, I guess, but catch up.

My mom was still doing very well when I moved home. My father was failing somewhat. We brought mom into the Wagon Wheel until a week or so before she died at the age of 97. She'd push some of her food away at the assisted living facility, but there was no stopping her when she got Kevin's pancakes. He'd put ears on the pancakes for her, just like Mickey Mouse. It was her favorite meal.

I was very proud to bring my mom back to where I hung out as a teenager. Kevin would always come over and talk to her. He'd call her "Mom," and she would say to me, "Is that the guy that used to run this restaurant?" "No, Mom," I'd say, "You're thinking about Kevin's dad, Wally." Then she'd say, "He sure looks a lot like his dad." And he does.

Coming back to Mankato was exciting in a way, even though I would have bet $10,000 to anyone that I would have never returned and lived here. But I'm so glad I did. The beaches, the mountains, and the night life of California were all good, but I'm more interested now in being here and deciding at two o'clock in the afternoon to hook up the boat and go sunfishing.

I've come full circle, and I am home again. This is it for me.

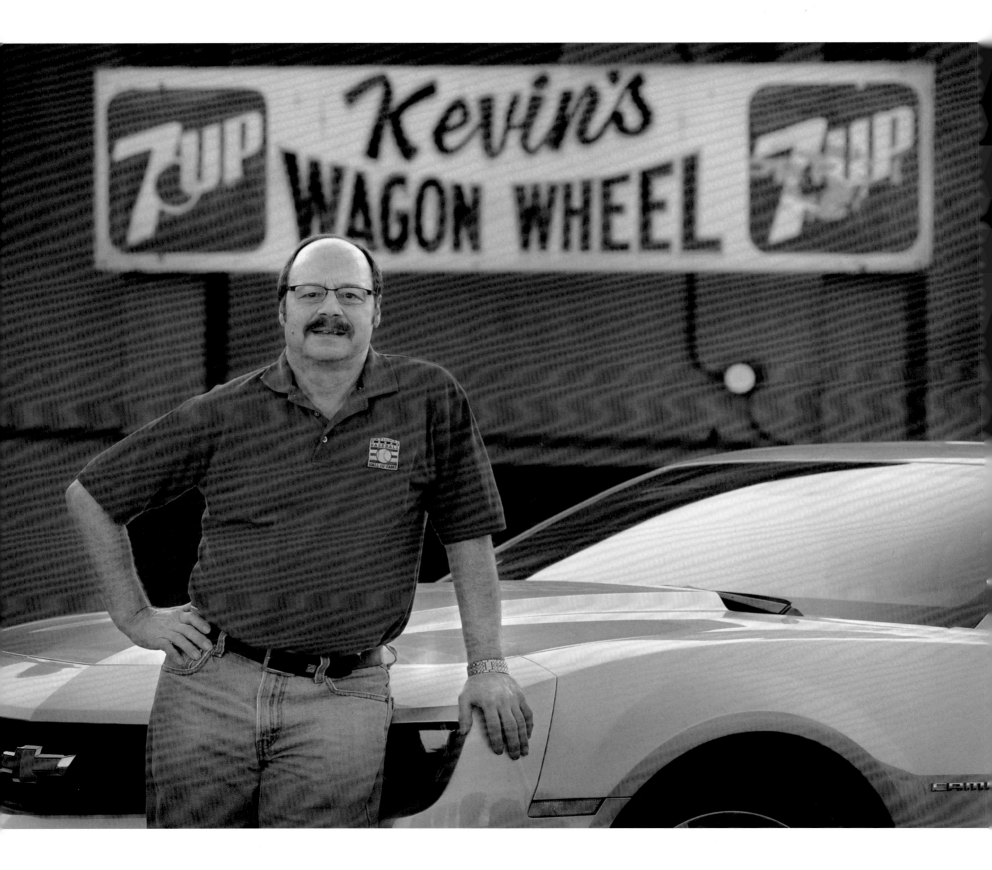

Kevin Haefner

My parents bought the Wagon Wheel in 1951. I come from a family of five boys and two girls, and most everybody worked here once upon a time. I was the only one who really showed an interest and stuck with it. I bought the place from my dad in 1983.

I'm here at 5:00 a.m. Monday through Saturday. It gets tough sometimes, but you just grin and bear it and plug on through it. I try to keep everything going at a smooth pace, talk to the customers, and make them feel at home. Remember somebody's birthday or something like that. It's just people things.

I have a responsibility, I feel, to my mother and father to keep the Wagon Wheel going. They worked hard at it, and I feel a responsibility to keep it a "happening" place—a place where people want to come to have a good time, maybe spout off at me a little, or whatever.

The people that I think need a little encouragement for the day, I try to banter a little at them, maybe smart off at them some. I try to make them feel that they're special, you know, because some people don't have it as good as other people.

Seventy-five percent of the people are in three or four times a week or more. Some are in two or three times a day. We try to keep everything reasonable so people come back—a good meal at a fair price. A lot of people don't have all the money in the world, so they like to get a good bargain—like today's special was chicken rice hotdish with salad and a roll for four dollars and sixty cents—your beverage included.

It makes me feel good when I hear some of the things people say about the Wagon Wheel. Knowing this place matters to people makes each day worth getting up for, I guess. I just try to be a person in the community that gives people a little boost. Not everybody has an opportunity like that—to make a difference. Some people just struggle every day.

I don't want any praise for what I do. I don't need that. I don't want that. I'm just an ordinary guy. I don't look down on too many people, and I don't look up at too many people either. People are people.

Wagon Wheel Timeline

1940 . . . . Wagon Wheel Café appears in Mankato City Directory for the first time

1951 . . . . Wally and Darlene Haefner purchase the Wagon Wheel from Albert and Arnold Bell

1952 . . . . Kevin Haefner born on January 10

1960 . . . . KEYC TV begins broadcasting in Mankato

1960–1961 . . . . Highway 169 rerouted, taking most traffic off Front Street

1968 . . . . Wagon Wheel completely remodeled (the last major changes to restaurant)

1968 . . . . Madison East Mall opens on Mankato's hilltop
(first major retail development away from downtown)

1975 . . . . Preparatory construction begins on downtown mall
(much of Front Street leveled to make way for the mall that now sits on what was once Front Street)

1978 . . . . Mankato Mall opens downtown

1982 . . . . Darlene Haefner passes away

1983 . . . . Kevin Haefner purchases Wagon Wheel from his father,
Wally, who continues helping out at the restaurant

1986 . . . . Veterans Memorial Bridge opens in downtown Mankato

1992 . . . . River Hills Mall opens on Mankato's hilltop

1992 . . . . Bretts and JC Penney, the last two major department stores downtown,
leave the downtown Mankato Mall

1993 . . . . Wagon Wheel eliminates evening meals and begins current hours—
Monday–Friday 6 a.m.–4 p.m. and Saturday 6 a.m.–1:30 p.m.

1993 . . . . Wally retires from the Wagon Wheel

2010 . . . . Kevin Haefner allows staff to place his photo next to Wally's photo on the back wall of the
Wagon Wheel (pictured left: Wally & Kevin Haefner)

Bullshippers Coffee Group

Several profiles in the book feature members of the coffee group that calls itself the "Bullshippers." Because of the group's longevity and importance to this project, the names of all members, present and past, are included here. The group organizes its list of active members by birthdays, and we've done the same.

Active members as of August 2012

Royal Lee (August 28, 1916)
Paul Meyer (May 18, 1918)
Gordon Beito (September 24, 1918)
Erv Kurth (September 20, 1920)
John Berg (January 3, 1923)
Dean Lowe (February 17, 1924)
Kelly Gage (June 20, 1925)
Chuck Heaberlin (October 1, 1925)
John Marso (November 23, 1927)
John Ehleringer (February 13, 1928)
Jerry Olinger (March 21, 1929)
Bob Layman (July 7, 1929)
Jerry Hansen (September 3, 1929)
Bob Browne (May 20, 1931)
Dick Towner (September 6, 1931)
Bob Anderson (September 7, 1931)
Frank Brown (December 8, 1931)
Jim Rossow (February 3, 1935)
Ray Beal (June 20, 1935)
Jim Borseth (April 1, 1937)
Bob Carlson (April 26, 1938)

Deceased members as of August 2012

Ken Berg
Fred Buscher
Merril Claridge
Dave Dallenbach
Ray Eckes
Phil Forrey
Larry Fowler
Bill Gushurst
Gordon Hakes
Vern Hanson
Harlan Held
Claude Howard
Russ Johnson
Med Jones
Kenneth Krause
Rollin Lander
Bob Lincoln
Roy Marks
Hub Mehr
Bill Morgan
Art Mornes
Stan Neubert
Bob Otto
Harold Paulsen
Frank Richardson
Harve Rivard
Harold Stevens
Morgan Thomas
Cleon Tollefsrud
Brad Troost

Wagon Wheel Index

Aaker, Don	121
Anderson, Eric	83
Bauer, Jean	21
Beck, Lisa	101
Bents, Dennis	119
Berg, John	71
Blekestad, Sandie	111
Bottin, Dave	103
Breitkreutz, Jerry	19
Brown, Frank	61
Browne, Bob	63
Buchanan, Marc	85
Bullshippers Coffee Group	131
Cassem, Marty	15
Coonce, Harry B.	41
DeWitte, Kenny	115
Dinsmore, Dan	75
Dorn, John	79
Dorn, Kathy	79
Fasnacht, Michelle	89
Foster, Rob	73
Garvin, Laurel	43
Green, Emily	75
Haefner, Kevin	127
Haney-White, Alissa	93
Hansen, Jerry	69
Hardt, Kenneth	29
Harkins, Elaine	33
Harrington, John	39
Johnson, Dan	91
Johnson, Jean	109
Johnson, Lowell	109
Kurth, Erv	55
Lee, Royal	53
Marso, John	65
Mehlhop, Harlan	45
Meyer, Paul	59
Miller, Rebel	95
Milner, Carole	23
Neilsen, Bill	9
Nickel, Joel "Augie"	25
Otto, Wes	11
Pfau, Jim	123
Phillips, Tammy	113
Piepho, Mark	81
Premeau, Denise	99
Schuck, Jerry	125
Sonnek, Paul	13
Spore, Ruth	31
Vaubel, Dolores	35
Wagon Wheel as a Community Gathering Place, The	4
Wagon Wheel Timeline	129
Walker, Brad	105
Wells, Randy	51
Wilcox, Cortnee	49
Wilcox, Ted	49

Kevin Haefner (left) has owned and operated the Wagon Wheel Restaurant in downtown Mankato for 15 years. Longtime employees from left are Denise Blaness, Barb Wendt and Geri Decker.

Free Press February 3, 1997

Regulars keep Wagon Wheel rolling

202 East Jackson Street
Post Office Box 3368
Mankato, Minnesota 56002-3368

Stan T. Christ
Mayor

(507) 387-8693
Fax: (507) 387-8642

City of MANKATO

Congratulations Kevin, to you & the crew! Stan

Applauze
Best of...
RESTAURANTS 2007

BEST DINER

WAGON WHEEL – MANKATO

WAGON WHEEL CAFÉ

EGGS
(any style)

2 Eggs: ham, bacon, (or)
  sausage, american fries,
  toast.......................4.00

2 Eggs: ham, bacon, (or)
  sausage, toast............3.25

2 Eggs: american fries,
  toast........................2.75

2 Eggs: with toast..........2.00

1 Egg: ham, bacon, (or)
  sausage, american fries,
  toast........................3.50

1 Egg: ham, bacon, (or)
  sausage, toast............3.00

1 Egg: american fries,
  toast........................2.60

2 Eggs: 5oz. steak,
  american fries,
  toast........................7.00

SIDE ORDERS

1 Egg......................1.00
American Fries or
  Hash Browns.........1.60
Ham, Bacon, or
  Sausage................2.00
Toast......................1.00
Muffin....................1.05
1 Pancake...............1.25
1 slice French Toast...1.25
Peanut Butter..........0.25
Bagel w/cream cheese...1.17

OMELETS
(includes toast)

Everything Omelet 3.50
*ham, cheese, onion,
green pepper*

Ham and Cheese 3.25
*diced ham and
american cheese*

Cheese 2.50
american cheese

PANCAKES

2 Cakes and 2 eggs: 3.50

2 Cakes, ham, bacon,
  or sausage: 3.50

Short Stack: 2 cakes: ...2.50

FRENCH TOAST

2 slices and 2 eggs: 3.50

2 slices and ham, bacon,
  or sausage: 3.50

2 slices: 2.50

CEREAL
(with milk)

Bran Flakes...............2.10
Corn Flakes..............2.10
Hot Oatmeal.............2.10

BEVERAGES

Coffee or Tea............1.17
Milk....................0.85 - 1.50
  (Whole, 2%, skim, or
  chocolate)
Juice.................1.30 - 2.00
Hot Chocolate..........1.17
Hot Spiced Cider.......1.17

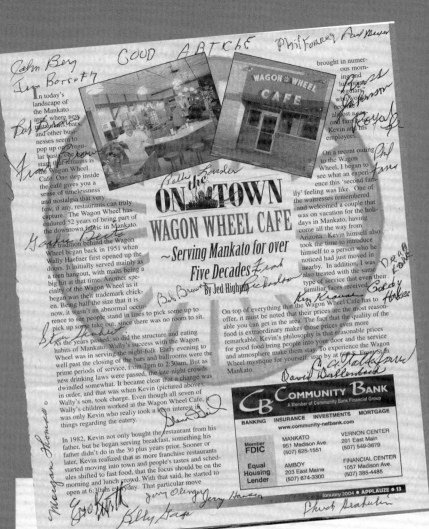

ON the TOWN
WAGON WHEEL CAFE
~ Serving Mankato for over Five Decades
By Jed Highum

In today's landscape of the Mankato area, where new restaurants, bars, and other businesses seem to pop up on a regular basis, one spot that remains is the Wagon Wheel Cafe. One step inside the café gives you a sense of timelessness and nostalgia that very few, if any, restaurants can truly capture. The Wagon Wheel has endured 52 years of being part of the downtown fabric in Mankato.

The tradition behind the Wagon Wheel began back in 1951 when Wally Haefner first opened up the doors. It initially served mainly as a teen hangout, with malts being a big hit at that time. Another specialty of the Wagon Wheel as it began was their trademark chicken. Being half the size that it is now, it wasn't an abnormal occurrence to see people stand in lines to pick some up to pick up some take out, since there was no room to sit.

As the years passed, so did the structure and eating habits of Mankato. Wally's success with the Wagon Wheel was in serving the night-folk. Early evening to well past the closing of the bars and ballrooms were the prime periods of service, from 7pm to 2:30am. But as new drinking laws were passed, the late-night crowds dwindled somewhat. It became clear that a change was in order, and that was when Kevin (pictured above), Wally's son, took charge. Even though all seven of Wally's children worked at the Wagon Wheel Cafe, it was only Kevin who really took a keen interest in things regarding the eatery.

In 1982, Kevin not only bought the restaurant from his father, but he began serving breakfast, something his father didn't do in the 30 plus years prior. Sooner or later, Kevin realized that as more franchise restaurants started moving into town and people's tastes and schedules shifted to fast food, that the focus should be on the morning and lunch crowd. With that said, he started to open at 6:30am everyday. That particular move brought in numerous morning and lunch "regulars" who become almost a second family to Kevin and his employees.

On a recent outing to the Wagon Wheel, I began to see what an experience this 'second family' feeling was like. One of the waitresses remembered and welcomed a couple that was on vacation for the holidays in Mankato, having come all the way from Arizona. Kevin himself also took the time to introduce himself to a person who he noticed had just moved in nearby. In addition, I was also treated with the same type of service that even their familiar faces received.

On top of everything that the Wagon Wheel Cafe has to offer, it must be noted that their prices are the most reasonable you can get in the area. The fact that the quality of the food is extraordinary makes those prices even more remarkable. Kevin's philosophy is that reasonable prices for good food bring people into your door and the service and atmosphere make them stay. To experience the Wagon Wheel mystique for yourself, stop by at 610 S. Front St. in Mankato.

CB Community Bank
A Member of Community Bank Financial Group
BANKING INSURANCE INVESTMENTS MORTGAGE
www.community-netbank.com

Member FDIC
MANKATO 951 Madison Ave. (507) 625-1551
AMBOY 203 East Maine (507) 674-3300

Equal Housing Lender
VERNON CENTER 201 East Main (507) 549-3679
FINANCIAL CENTER 1057 Madison Ave. (507) 385-4485

January 2004 • APPLAUZE • 13

Wagon Wheel Café

Ranch Steak $5.00
Tenderized Steak, Onion Rings, French Fries, Salad, Toast

Steak Sandwich $5.00
5 oz. Sirloin Steak, French Fries, Toast

Chicken Strips $5.00
3 Strips, French Fries, Salad, Toast

Bonanza Burger $3.50
Jumbo Burger, French Fries, Coleslaw

Chicken Drummies . . . $5.00
5 Drummies, French Fries, Salad, Toast

DINNERS
Strip Sirloin $6.25
Wagon Wheel Steak . . . 6.00
1/2 Chicken 6.25
1/4 Chicken 4.75
Jumbo Shrimp 5.75
2 Pork Chops 6.75
Ham Dinner 4.75
Fish Steak 4.75
Hamburger Steak 5.00

(Choice of Potato and Salad, French Fries, American Fries, Hash Browns, Mashed Potatoes, Cole Slaw, Cottage Cheese, Jello, Lettuce Salad)

1/4 Chicken and Toast . . $3.75
All Substitutions Extra

Grilled Chicken Breast . . $4.25
Cottage Cheese and Jello, Slice of Whole Wheat Toast

Cold Plate $4.00
Ham Sandwich, macaroni or potato salad, and Jello

SANDWICHES
B.L.T. $2.40
Fried Ham 1.90
Chip Steak 1.90
Denver 1.95
Ham Salad 1.80
Fishwich 1.95
Tuna Salad 2.00
Egg Salad 2.00
Grilled Cheese 1.75
Grilled Ham and Cheese . 2.30
Chicken Sandwich . . . 2.40

California Burger . . . $1.95
Cheeseburger 1.80
Bacon Cheeseburger . . 2.40
Hamburger 1.50
Jumbo Hamburger . . . 1.95
Patty Melt 2.40
Beef Sandwich 2.40
Braunschweiger . . . 1.75
Cheese Sandwich . . . 1.75
Fried Egg 1.75

SALADS
Coleslaw $1.25
Lettuce 1.25
Salad Bowl 1.80
Small Chef 2.60
Large Chef 4.00
Cottage Cheese/Fruit . . 1.80
Potato Salad (seasonal) . . 1.75

French Fries $1.35
Onion Rings 1.75
Home-Made Pie 1.35

SOUP
Home-Made Bean Soup . . $1.50
Soup-of-the-Day 1.50
Chili 1.85

BEVERAGES
Coffee or Tea . . . . . $ .97
Milk . . . . . .85 and 1.10
Juice . . . . 1.00 and 1.75
Hot Chocolate 97
Shakes 2.25

Small Pop . . . . . . $ .70
Large Pop 93
Ice Tea 93
Lemonade (seasonal) . . .93